Children and Music

Children
and
Music

Atarah Ben-Tovim

A handbook for parents,
teachers and others
interested in the musical
welfare of children

Adam & Charles Black · London

First published 1979
by A. & C. Black (Publishers) Ltd
35 Bedford Row, London WC1R 4JH

ISBN 0 7136 1960 0

Ben-Tovim Atarah
    Children and music.
    1. Music – Instruction and study –
Great Britain
    I. Title
    780'.72941   MT3.G7
    ISBN 0–7136–1960–0

Filmset by Keyspools Ltd, Golborne, Lancs.
Printed in Great Britain by
Hollen Street Press Ltd, Slough, Berks.

Contents

Photography by Douglas Boyd
Reproduced by permission of Children's Concert Centre archives

Section 1
Why Learn a Musical Instrument?

The ability to appreciate music is a lifelong enrichment of leisure time.

Yet, music is the most technical, least verbal or representational art-form. It has no shape, no mass; it is invisible and intangible. It even has its own language. You may read a million words about music and still know no more about it than when you began.

Perhaps this doesn't matter. After all, anyone can listen to the wonderful tunes of Dvořák's New World Symphony or Tchaikovsky's ballet music and enjoy them on an instinctive and emotional level, without knowing a bass clef from a bar-line. That is part of the wonder of music.

But music has far more to offer, and to progress from simply enjoying a good tune to *understanding* music is an immense and highly worthwhile task.

Musical criticism, musicology, biographies of great musicians are interesting but peripheral. They teach you nothing about *music*.

There is only one way to come to understand music: by learning to play a musical instrument, whether an external one like the piano or flute or by training the human voice to become an instrument.

This is a process on two levels: consciously, one learns to operate the instrument, studies the grammar and syntax of music, reading notation, observing rhythm, and appreciating melody and harmony; concurrently, the subconscious mind is digesting all these elements to form an awareness and comprehension of the art-form which is music.

From the viewpoint of most adults, that is the most important reason for studying a musical instrument. Those who have studied an instrument, however long ago (and regardless of how much they think they have forgotten), have an insight into music far beyond what can be gained from a lifetime of unsupported listening.

By its nature, that is a long-term benefit, but there is also a host of short-term ones, too. As a teacher of twenty year's experience, it remains to me a constantly recurring miracle to witness the mental, physical and spiritual development of a child who is truly learning a musical instrument.

What are these other benefits?

The benefit of "something to do"

> "Practising is quite nice, really. Some of my friends are jealous because, when they're just messing about, I've got something to do." (Danielle, aged 10: Grade 3 clarinet)★

Every parent knows how important it is to have a constructive answer to the perennial question: "What can I do?" How nice – for both parent and child – to have a worthwhile answer!

I often ask children whether they mind having to practise regularly, each day. The point of this question is to find out whether they are on the right instrument. If they are, then the answer usually accords with Danielle's. She is not what you would call a "musical child", but she is on the right instrument and enjoys her daily practice for the very good reason that it gives her "something to do".

Not only does it fill some otherwise empty time, but it leaves her with the feeling of having done something instead of just messing about.

People used to say that children should be seen and not heard. Today's updated version of that cliché is the belief that as long as children are doing something, it doesn't really matter what. This fails to take into account the big difference between the way in which children want to spend their leisure time and the general desire of adults to "switch off" after a day's work or at the end of the week. Children don't have this need to switch off. Given a genuine choice, most children will prefer to do something productive with free time, rather than just sitting passively watching television, or messing about.

The benefit of achievement

> "I've taken four exams so far – Step One, Step Two, Step Three and Grade 1. They're very easy exams, but I think they're quite important because it proves you've got somewhere." (Susannah, aged 10: Grade 1 piano)

★ This and the following quotations are from interviews with children recorded by Atarah for her Radio 3 series "Atarah's Music Box".

Achievement is a vital factor in developing the character of any child. Any process to which a child devotes continuing effort should provide a succession of achievements.

Learning a musical instrument fulfils this need to a very high degree. Music is so technically assessable that, from the very first notes played by a child, through scales and simple tunes to "real music", it is always possible – indeed it is vitally necessary – for the child to assess his own progress. Hearing with his own ears that he can do today what he was unable to do a week ago, and knowing that this progress is the direct result of the work put in, gives any child a real sense of achievement and an appreciation of the value of work.

The benefit of balanced development

"When you first play tunes, it's very difficult to hold your instrument properly and remember to breathe at the right time. You've got to play the right notes of course, and count properly, too.

"Even when you can do all that, you're not really playing music unless you try to make the right kind of sound ... That's very difficult ... You don't have to do that sort of thing at school, ever." (Michelle, aged 11 : Grade 3 flute)

In academic education there is an inevitable imbalance between mental activity and physical inactivity. Physical education develops physique and improves co-ordination but does little for the intellect or the soul.

There is only one occupation open to most children which offers the possibility of developing mind, body and soul in balance: learning to play an instrument.

Playing an instrument is far more *physical* than many non-players realise and it is impossible to learn what has to be learnt without considerable *mental* application. Yet, a proper course of instrumental instruction benefits not only the body and the brain; it has a great bonus in that the child learns to make aesthetic judgements. Such judgements are not made by flexing the muscles, nor by any process of logical deduction. They are made by what has to be called: the *soul*.

There are techniques to measure development of physique and mental progress, but it is difficult, if not impossible, to measure the development of a child's soul. Yet, you can say to a very young pupil: "That was technically right, but play it with more feeling." And the child will play the same passage again, technically the same, *but with more feeling*!

The benefits of discipline and self-discipline

"The harp is such a complicated instrument that I have to practise about three-quarters of an hour each day. You can't miss even one day because you go stale and when you try to play the harp again, your fingers get lost among all those strings." (Harriet, aged 12: Grade 4 harp)

"I work at it for perhaps half an hour every day. The trouble is that you have to play the same things each day. If you didn't, you wouldn't get any better. And I want to get better, so I do." (Rachel, aged 8: beginner on violin)

From the first lesson, the child has to realise that most of the work of learning cannot be fitted into the weekly half-hour with the teacher. It has to be accomplished between lessons, by regular practising. Initially, parental support will help, but eventually, the child is on his own.

A child who has learnt to discipline himself in one sphere of activity finds that he can apply this self-management technique in other spheres, with a consequent all-round benefit to his powers of concentration.

The benefit of being able to play

"Looking back on it, I suppose I did get bored at times. You know, doing scales and simple tunes at the beginning. But now, it's fantastic. I play regularly in the school band and in an amateur symphony orchestra. We're doing Beethoven's Fifth at the moment, which is about as square as you can get. And it's not exactly exciting for the trombone, because we don't come in till the last movement, but I like some orchestral music.

"Two nights a week, I play with a local jazz band, improvising. In fact, I seem to enjoy playing all kinds of music. I just like playing." (Adrian, aged 14: Grade 8 trombone)

The ability to play is a lifelong source of pleasure. Whether you are re-creating the masterpiece of a great composer, giving meticulous care to every single note as written, or whether you are improvising

Atarah coaching beginner flautists

as the spirit moves, being able to make music by playing an instrument is a joy far greater than non-players can understand.

The benefit of playing with others

> "I joined the quintet because it's an excuse to form close relationships with the other girls . . . It feels really good to be in a group of people doing something you're all good at together." (Jane, aged 14: playing in a wind quintet)

> "I know it looks funny: a girl like me carrying a great big double-bass around, but the great thing about being a bass-player is that lots of people want you to play with them. There are never enough bass-players, so really, playing the double-bass has made me quite popular." (Vera, aged 16: Grade 8 double-bass)

Some lucky children never have any problem making friends, in or out of school. Others find it a boon that their ability to play an instrument makes them desirable to groups of children who need a bass for the school orchestra, a clarinet for a wind quintet, or whatever.

It's nice to be wanted . . .

The benefit of therapy

"I was getting into trouble . . . You know, nicking stuff in shops and that . . . with some other boys. Then I got my electric guitar. It was a rotten guitar, really, but it got me started.

"I don't go round with the gang any more. I practise for two hours a day, usually, so I don't have time to . . . you know, mess about like that." (John, aged 14. At 16, he obtained his Grade 5 on classical guitar!)

Not all children want to belong to groups, like Vera and Jane. The child who is happiest on his own can learn to make music alone, on

Music helps to make like-minded friends

the piano or classical guitar, for instance. Having something so very positive and rewarding to do is a great relief from loneliness for solitary children.

In that way, learning an instrument can be a general therapy for many children who are not in any obvious way "disturbed". Yet the process can also be a very potent specific therapy for children who *are* disturbed. If more musicians went into the probation and psychiatric services, we should discover much more about the use of music as deliberate therapy in this way.

John was an adolescent boy who was emotionally disturbed. He was introduced to the guitar by a guitar-playing educational psychologist who concentrated upon the toughness and manliness of playing the instrument. He exploited the images and heroes of the pop world, guessing that John, like most children, was secretly dreaming of becoming a rock star overnight.

Eventually, John decided for himself that he needed proper lessons on classical guitar in order to improve his technique. He started to spend an hour a day working on his classical guitar as well as more than two hours improvising on his electric guitar.

The result – whether or not he ever gets to be a rock star – is not only that he has no time for the anti-social behaviour of the past, but also that he has discovered how to work hard at something, with consequent improvement in most of his school-work.

The benefit of understanding music

Music is all around us today. Yet, for those who have not learned to understand music, its ubiquity brings no clarity. To give a metaphor from another art-form, it is as if they spend their lives surrounded by wonderful paintings, each covered by an obscuring veil. Learning to play an instrument is the metaphorical scissors which would enable them to cut through the veil and see in brilliant clarity the details of the artist's composition and intent.

Conclusion

In addition to the twin benefits of being able to play music in a way no non-player can hope to do, this process of learning an instrument gives children "something to do", it provides a sense of achievement, it teaches self-discipline, it helps them to make like-minded friends and it is a powerful therapy for all sorts of childhood conditions. It develops body, brain and soul in balance.

And . . . it's fun!

Why, you might wonder, have so few children been able to obtain all these benefits?

The answer is a sad one: for no good reason, there has evolved the Musical Obstacle Race, which is so designed that most children cannot get to the finishing line and collect the benefits to which they are entitled. Indeed, *most* children are not allowed to get as far as the start.

Section 2
The Musical Obstacle Course

There is nothing wrong with obstacle races in themselves. Properly designed, they are series of filters which ensure that only the fittest reach the finishing line.

But the Musical Obstacle Course is a hybrid; it was never planned; it has grown up haphazardly; one part bears no relation to another; it is unfair, some of the hurdles constantly allowing the wrong runners to pass – others deflecting most of them off the track irrevocably.

Because it is such an untidy complex of obstacles, the course has not been identified as such. Therefore its effects on the young runners have not been analysed. The analysis could only be carried out by musically-educated people, but few musicians are in a position to see more than one hurdle at a time, let alone appreciate the cumulative effect of the several hurdles. So much time and effort goes into equipping oneself musically to become an orchestral player, an instrumental teacher, a session musician or whatever, that we musicians do not "chop and change" very much in our careers. We tend to stick to one aspect of music, with all the limitations of perspective which that implies.

My own beginnings in music were conventional and hedged about with prejudice in favour of classical music and the instruments on which it is played. But I have had an unusually varied career for a musician. It is this variety of experience which has given me a ticket for the metaphorical grandstand, from which I can see most, if not all, of the course.

As well as being a teacher, an orchestral principal for twelve years and a solo performer, I devise and present concerts and music shows designed to make all kinds of music relevant and fun for modern children. While researching for newspaper and magazine articles and preparing radio and television programmes, I have interviewed and worked with children from all social and educational backgrounds (and their teachers) and learned much about the workings of the course. So, join me in the grandstand and see, firstly, what the course should look like *without obstacles*.

First, the start!

The starter's gun should be audible to all. In musical terms, it should be possible for every child to be equally *inspired* with an instinctive enjoyment of music and motivated by this inspiration to take the first few steps along the course. Resting on the starting blocks in a posture of cultural passivity – listening to tunes, playing with recorders and simple percussion instruments, strumming guitars and singing – is very pleasant. But, if you're not allowed to hear the gun of inspiration, you'll never leave the blocks.

Once up and running, the first lap is finding somewhere the parents of the child, the non-specialist teacher (or the child himself, if he is old enough) can go for unbiased *guidance and advice* in choosing the right instrument, finding an instrument to learn on, finding a teacher, and guidance in the direction of the kind of music in which the child is most interested.

In the ideal situation, the people providing this help and guidance will have been trained for the job. They will be devoid of unproductive or negative musical prejudice and unable to say, for example, that one kind of music is better than another or that classical instruments are more valid than electric ones. They will not regard themselves as failed musicians or unsuccessful performers because they will have been taught that their vocation as musical counsellors is self-justifying and certainly no less important to the community than playing in a symphony orchestra or writing music that few audiences will ever hear.

The next lap in this perfect race will find the child enjoying the facilities provided by the community for music as a *leisure* activity and rejoicing in the ability to walk at any reasonable hour into a properly equipped and staffed musical leisure centre, in the same way as one can walk into a public library or the local swimming-pool.

The child who has devoted so much time, energy and concentration to studying the complex subject of music, by learning an instrument, should have his achievement recognised by the educational system, by being entitled to 'O' and 'A' level passes both in Performing on the Instrument and in Musical Theory and History. This is a direct parallel with taking English Language and English Literature or Art and the History of Art. There are welcome moves in this direction.

And how does the course end?

The ideal course does not have one common finishing line for all runners. The important thing is that each child should be able to reach his own finishing line: the point at which he can attain his share of the benefits of learning a musical instrument.

Why most children lose out on music

If we now compare this ideal course with present reality – the Obstacle Course – we can identify five important hurdles:

> a general *lack of inspiration*, vital to make music accessible and relevant to all children;
>
> a *lack of guidance* for parents, non-specialist teachers and children;
>
> a *lack of facilities* for the pursuit of music as a leisure activity;
>
> a *lack of recognition* by the educational system;
>
> *prejudice and bias.*

There is a host of smaller hurdles, but these are clustered around one or other of the main ones.

Lack of inspiration

Any music-lover knows that live performance is what music is all about. Broadcast relays, records and cassettes are poor echoes of the experience of live music. Why, then, are live concerts for children not regarded as the most potent source of inspiration and treated with all the care which that merits? So often, a child's first visit to a live musical performance fails to be an exciting and enlightening trip into another world. And why?

The sad reason is that so many "children's concerts" are ill-conceived, badly thought-out, sloppily presented and performed by musicians who regard working for children either as a boring chore to be undergone strictly for cash or as a rare chance of indulging their egos in ways which no adult audience would tolerate.

Every time a musician, teacher, conductor or presenter seeks to foist his own prejudices on modern, media-educated children, he is not only doomed to failure, he is guilty of the crime of driving children away from everything except the commercial world of pop which welcomes them with open arms and waiting cash-registers.

We may not like – indeed, some of us may deplore – the modern ubiquity of pop and background music. Yet, if we denigrate the culture with which all children are familiar, we not only risk alienating them, we are blindly and deafly turning our backs on the social phenomenon of the pop revolution which, for the first time ever, has brought music into the lives of *all* children.

It is a musical tragedy that we have failed to seize this wonderful opportunity to lead every child on to more enriching musical experiences.

The images and heroes of the pop culture are a powerful source of inspiration and motivation to learn about music. Why should it be ignored or denigrated by prejudiced parents, teachers, and musicians?

And why are so many children's music programmes on radio and television either inanely pop-orientated or simply boring? Why do so many people talk so patronisingly to children about their own musical prejudices? Why should we assume that the next generation should share our preferences even if presented *without* bias?

Why is peer-group approval and the natural phenomenon of children hero-worshipping older schoolmates not utilised and harnessed as a source of inspiration?

Why does the arts establishment in Great Britain dismiss this whole field of activity as being "educational", while the educational establishment retorts that it is artistic, in a shabby Catch-22 of mutual blame-shifting?

Does this situation need to continue?

> "I don't like music. They took us to the . . . . Orchestra at the . . . . Hall. All the school had to go because it was free. Some of the boys flew paper aeroplanes down on to the kids below . . . one boy spent the whole time in the lavatory." (Stephen, aged 10: interviewed on his concert-going experience!)

Lack of guidance for parents, non-specialist teachers and children

Even if a parent, an interested non-specialist teacher, or the child himself manages to find a source of inspiration, where does he go for the all-important help and guidance on choosing the right instrument, to find an instrument to play on, and to find the right teacher?

In Britain today, it is virtually impossible to obtain this guidance. The result? Every year, hundreds of thousands of children, rightly with high expectations, start to learn musical instruments. Eight out of ten find they get nowhere and give up, feeling frustrated and that they are "no good at music".

In many cases they have been persuaded to take up the wrong instrument in the first place. The adults who have been advising them are amateurs in what should be a specialised field: that of matching each child with the right instrument for his mental, physical and emotional make-up. If a musical counselling service were available at this stage, the failure ratio would be inverted and eight out of ten would succeed and go on to a full enjoyment of music as a leisure activity.

But there is no such counselling service available. Nobody is employed by the community or is in business privately to act as a Musical Advice Bureau. There is no training for the vocation of musical counsellor.

It was largely to fight this lack that we set up the Bentovim Children's Music Centre, but we are a privately-financed Charitable Trust with no public subsidy and the number of children we can help, and the number of students we can train, is small compared with the hundreds of thousands of frustrated children who slip dispiritedly each year down the musical drain.

"I wanted to learn the guitar, but the music teacher said they needed another trumpet for the band. So they made me start the trumpet. I did try for a bit, but I just wasn't any good at music."

"We'd like to help Debbie, but we don't know anything about music. Her teacher thinks she'd be able to learn an instrument. Her Grandma has offered to pay for piano lessons, but Debbie doesn't like the piano, so we don't know what to do."

". . . is quite an intelligent boy for his age and seems to have some musical talent. He has been teaching himself the guitar and has made surprising progress. How can we persuade him to take up a more worthwhile instrument?"

These are just three of the thousands of requests for guidance I receive each year. Here are three more:

"How does one go about finding a teacher?"

"Where can we find a list of suitable courses for our son, aged thirteen?"

"Where is the nearest Rock Workshop?"

And three more:

"How can we tell whether to trust the local music shop and accept the owner's advice? Surely he just wants to sell the most expensive instrument . . ."

"The school doesn't seem able to help. Apparently the music teacher doesn't even appear at some lessons. He doesn't answer our letters. The local Music Centre is only interested in children who can play instruments they need in the Saturday orchestra. Who is supposed to help people like us?"

"How much money should we have to spend on a first instrument?"

And three more:

"She has been making good progress, but seems to have run out of interest, if you know what I mean. Should we change her teacher? What can we do to revive her interest in music?"

"I was forced to practise, but this approach seems to be old-fashioned. Should you make children practise, today?"

"Where can we get a list of musical holidays for the whole family to go on?"

Requests from all social backgrounds and people of all ages:

"... the kids like us. That's what it's all about. You don't need to read music and play Beethoven, to be a good group ... Some days we're quite good ... it depends how we feel. How do we find a manager to get us some gigs? We've been playing our instruments for more than six months now and I think what we need is ... exposure ..."

"... request your help in finding a musical career for our daughter. We should like her to be a professional musician on the flute or another woodwind instrument. Can she start soon? Is it a good idea to begin on the recorder? She is eighteen months old and we don't want to leave it too late ..."

And, lastly, in a letter (!):

"How should I breathe?"

Lack of musical leisure facilities

Every Local Authority in Britain has a statutory duty to provide leisure facilities for its area. As in all politics, of course, there is a catch: it's up to the local councillors to define what is meant by "leisure" and then what the facilities should be.

While a football-mad councillor will leap up and down demanding new goal-posts at every meeting, the few music-lovers who do get involved in local politics admit defeat at the outset by taking it for granted that the community will not provide facilities for their interest, which they believe to be a minority taste.

Perhaps nobody wants musical leisure facilities?

Perhaps there is no need for properly staffed and equipped places to which children could go at any reasonable hour to listen to music, to play alone or with others, or simply to meet others interested in music?

Nothing could be further from the truth. If, at an Atarah's Band concert, I ask two thousand *average* children how many are learning a musical instrument, about one-half of the audience will raise a hand. This doesn't mean that they are candidates for the Menuhin school. What most of them mean is that they're learning to play recorder, mouth-organ, simple percussion instruments, or to strum guitars under the guidance of non-specialist teachers. They're on the starting blocks, waiting for somewhere to go.

Of the one thousand children who put their hands up, about a hundred have benefited from the drive of parents, individual teachers and music advisers. These children come up to me after the concert and tell me how they're getting on with one lesson a week during term-time from a specialist teacher, either at school or privately. They're going somewhere. They're on the first lap of the course.

A few of the lucky hundred, depending entirely in which area they happen to live, will be able to take part in a Saturday morning orchestra, school orchestra, the junior section of a brass band, perhaps a junior dance band. Even if they are lucky enough to live in the catchment area of a Music Centre, this will be closed when most needed, during school holidays.

Remember that we started with one thousand out of two thousand children expressing an interest in *doing something* about music – not passively listening. It is natural for children to pursue hobbies in their spare time with tremendous energy and enthusiasm. Where can this one thousand children go to pursue their hobby?

Would any local councillor think it intelligent to have children learn to swim and then not provide a swimming-pool?

Would anyone suggest teaching children to read and then not having public libraries?

Would anyone suggest giving children sports lessons and then not having recreation grounds for them?

With one or two overburdened exceptions, there is nowhere for musically-interested children to go. For them, there is no equivalent of the swimming-pool, the library and the recreation ground.

"Sometimes you get very depressed playing on your own. There's only one lesson a week when you can even talk to someone ... about music. If only there was a kind of musical Youthie, you could get together with other kids who play ... even if they're not very good." (Philip, aged 13 : Grade 3 flute)

"The trouble with playing electric instruments with my friends is that there's nowhere for us to go normally – even to play together. And it's almost impossible for us to find the sort of help you get in an orchestra or playing chamber music ..." (Nick, aged 16 : synthesiser player)

Of course it would cost a little public money to make musical leisure centres where children (and adults) could go to enjoy all aspects of

Filming with John Noakes for BBC TV's "Blue Peter" programme in the Bentovim Children's Music Centre percussion studio

music and music-making. But traffic lights cost money. The public library costs money. The local swimming-pool costs money.

In fact, a musical leisure centre costs less than most other leisure facilities to make and run. Every town in Britain has – usually already purchased by the Council – old property with big rooms and solid walls which modern families do not want to live in. It is a shame to knock these buildings down and here is a purpose for which they are admirably suited. A sports centre, leisure hall or swimming-pool has to be purpose-built, whereas a music centre is best made by converting old buildings.

It isn't hard or very costly. My husband converted four adjacent houses into a sophisticated complex of musical leisure facilities for children. He did it in his own spare time during eighteen months.

We now have practice studios, a professional recording studio, rehearsal rooms, two recital rooms, a rock studio for electric instruments, an Asian studio, a listening room, a library, a canteen and a social area – as well as a specialist studio for each family of instruments. We run Open Days for children and parents who need the first guidance after inspiration. We run Day Schools for children, at all stages of learning, to enjoy master class situations with top-rate performing musicians. We're beginning to train students to get involved in these areas. Our next project is to run seminars and courses to help performers and students who want seriously to work in this field.

If we can do this as private individuals out of our own resources, what could not a Council achieve, using the thousands of unemployed school-leavers and the all-too-many skilled building workers who are on the dole?

Any Council or Arts Association could copy what we have done. Let's hope they will.

Lack of recognition by the educational establishment

Let's follow the progress of the lucky hundred children, some of whom will get as far on their instruments as, for example, Grade 5 on piano or guitar, or Grade 8 on the flute.

To do this, they will have put in no less work and achieved no less progress than their coevals who obtain 'O' level passes in English or Maths. On the contrary, they will have had to work a lot harder, because probably none of them will have had more than one period a week of tuition. All the rest of the work has had to be done on their own.

An objective educational system would reward all this application of effort and give the children some mark of recognition of their achievement.

Instead, instrumental performance is not, at the time of writing, recognised as a GCE 'O' level subject. It counts for a mean 10 to 20 per cent of the marks obtainable in the rather amorphous subject called: Music.

To explain to a non-musician what that means, you have to imagine the English Language examination being abolished and mastery of the English language counting for 10 to 20 per cent in the English Literature examination.

On reflection, the situation is even harsher, for the Music syllabus virtually ignores the development of musical forms after 1900, excluding jazz, pop, rock, folk and media music. So, perhaps, the

String master class at the Bentovim Children's Music Centre

parallel is to imagine an English literature paper concerned exclusively with medieval literature, written in a language which most modern children could not really understand.

This is a curious situation. Our present system of education is examination-orientated. The purpose of setting examinations and awarding certificates to those who pass them is to provide a simple and easily comprehensible method of evaluating the amount of work which a child has shown itself capable of doing in a particular subject or area of study. Nobody pretends that a child takes 'O' level English in order to become a writer, or 'A' level Physics in order to make H-bombs.

One would think that the more assessable the subject, the more useful it would be in such a system. There is no possible in-school or out-of-school activity more assessable than instrumental technique.

One can hope that this situation will change, but it remains fact that, however brilliant the young performer, however much application and discipline have gone into studying an instrument, it is not yet possible to achieve a single 'O' level certificate for instrumental performance.

The children about whom this book is written are not prodigies. They are average to bright children who have to work hard to achieve their musical results. All their parental and school training leads them to expect recognition – from parent and school – for this kind of hard work.

It's true that the best result of all the hard work is the eventual ability to play an instrument, but it remains bewildering to many children that the educational system acts the petty part of a betrayed parent and refuses them the rightful recognition which would provide both a goal to work for and a positive reward.

There might be some excuse for the delays if the educational administration had to start from scratch, in constructing a basis for examination and a complete set of standards, but this immense labour has already been done. There exists an excellent system of examinations in musical performance, conducted by the Associated Board of the Royal Schools of Music.

It would be fair, constructive and administratively practical to amend the Associated Board's system and award GCE 'O' level passes to children who had obtained an *amended* Grade 6 and 'A' level passes to those with an *amended* Grade 8.

Of course, within the musical fraternity, the achievement of a child in obtaining the existing Grade 6 or 8, is recognised, but the rest of the world pays attention only to GCE results. Prospective employers are unlikely to understand that a child who has obtained an existing Grade 6 on guitar has demonstrated a general level of intelligence and application otherwise evidenced by an 'O' level pass in, say, Mathematics or General Science.

"To get my Grade 8, I practised two hours every day ... with a private teacher. But at school – it's a new Comprehensive – the Music Teacher hasn't started the set works or harmony (three months before 'O' Levels), so I haven't a chance of getting Music 'O' Level because playing, however good I am, only counts for a few marks. It's not fair." (Fiona, aged 16: Grade 8 guitar)

Prejudice and bias

People have come to think that there is a Great Cultural Divide, with the majority of children on the pop side and most adults on the classical side. Many parents, teachers and musicians would subscribe to this belief, agreeing among themselves that it is a pity that children are on the "wrong" side of the abyss and regretting that there is apparently no way of bridging it and bringing them across to the "right" side.

The metaphor is wrong and misleading. There is no essential difference between listening to pop music and listening to classical music in the way that musically-uneducated people do – for simple pleasure.

It's worth noting that the term "classical music" is simply a label for the formal music which was written during the period starting with the younger Bachs at the beginning of the eighteenth century and ending more or less with Schubert's later works in the middle of the nineteenth century.

"Classical music" is abused to mean any *serious* music.

The origin of the Great Cultural Divide myth lies in the unquestioned assumption that serious music is "better" than light music; that even simply listening to serious music is somehow "better" than listening to light music.

As far as listening goes, it doesn't matter whether one is listening to Early Music, Baroque, Classical, Romantic, Modern, Folk – or Pop Music or Jazz – they are all music and to claim that Early Music is better than Jazz or that Classical Music is better than Pop is simply evidence of confused thinking. It's like saying that coffee is a better beverage than cocoa, or that tennis is better than swimming.

I'm not suggesting that musically-educated people should sit and listen only to pop music, any more than I should suggest feeding musically-uneducated children on classical symphonies...!

It is to me one of the wonders of the art-form that there are so many different kinds of music to suit different temperaments and indeed the same person at different moments. Someone who enjoys and respects only one kind of music is poorer than another person who can enjoy many kinds of music. At different times I can be moved to tears by a Mozart piano concerto or a folk song, uplifted by Mahler, or cheered up by Mancini.

And if we want to contact modern children and inspire them with an interest in *all* music, then we *must* exploit the music with which they are familiar. Only thus can we lead them on to discover that there are other kinds of music which they can also enjoy.

"I wanted to play the drums, but the music teacher said drums weren't a proper instrument and that only stupid boys played the drums. So, that was the end of that." (Wayne, aged 14 and "in trouble".)

"The last music lesson of term, the teacher said we could bring our own records to play to the class, so we all turned up with rock ... and punk and that sort of thing ... He did play some of our records, but most of the time he played records he liked ... He didn't like ours and we didn't like his." (Helen, aged 13: no instrument)

"I've been playing folk guitar now for about five years and writing my own songs. I take 'O' level music next term, so I think my songs aren't bad. At any rate, I perform quite a lot to public audiences and they seem to like them.

"The sort of material I sing is much more popular with the kids at school than what the school orchestra plays, but when I suggested to the music master that I could do a spot in the school concert, he just wouldn't listen." (Billy, aged 16: folk singer and guitarist)

"I like Joan Sutherland best. That's in classical music. But, in pop music, I like men best ... like David Essex ... and I like groups: Showaddywaddy and Mud and Rubettes and Queen and things like that." (Katherine, aged 11: singing and Grade 2 piano)

Conclusion

If we want to *contact* modern children, we must discard prejudice against what they like and bias in favour of what we like. To inspire them we must come to terms with the pop phenomenon, and use it as what it can be: a most powerful weapon for inspiring children towards music of *all* kinds ...

We must give them unbiased guidance to fulfil their individual musical needs, which may be different from ours.

We must give them musical leisure centres where they can enjoy and share this lifelong hobby.

We must give them the formal recognition which our exam-orientated society has taught them to expect.

Music has so many benefits for children that we *must* take down the obstacles which force so many children to lose out on music.

Section 3
Inspiring Children to Take an Interest in Music

The first major obstacle is the lack of inspiration. The child who is not inspired to an awareness of music will never get as far as the other hurdles.

Teachers, more than anybody else, will know that the vital stage before which no child begins to learn is that of inspiration. In terms of music this means that there has to be a "breathing in", a communication to the child that music is accessible and enjoyable and relevant to the child's life.

Motivation may follow, but, without inspiration, there is no beginning.

> "My brother played the violin and he liked playing in orchestras. I wanted to play in an orchestra like him, so I chose the bassoon." (Colin, aged 13 : Grade 4 bassoon)

Some children are fortunate enough to have parents or older brothers and sisters or other relatives or friends who are able to communicate to them, or inspire them with, their own excitement and joy at listening to, and making, music. This inspiration comes naturally, but the majority of children do not have this family help and support. For them, we have to work at the business of inspiration.

"We" should mean all adults who have already discovered music in our own lives. In the case of each individual child, it means the immediate family and the schoolteachers with whom he comes into contact. Parents who themselves lack a particular area of experience – whether it's music or something else – sometimes assume that teachers, because they're generally better educated, must automatically have the experience which the parents lack. This places a great burden on teachers – particularly non-specialist teachers who have in their charge children during the formative years when inspiration should be sought. To assume that a non-specialist teacher has superior knowledge of something as abstract and technical as music is frightening – for the teacher!

In addition to parents, non-specialist and specialist teachers, there are many other sources of inspiration: television and radio, records and cassettes, peer-group approval and peer-imitation, amateur music-making and professionally-performed concerts.

> "I went to a concert in Liverpool and saw a harpist . . . I just took a fancy to it." (Harriet, aged 11 : beginner harpist)

> "When I was six, I saw a television programme of Jack Parnell and his Big Band and I just liked the sound of the trumpet . . . so I decided to learn it." (Michaela, aged 9 : Grade 5 trumpet)

What can parents do?

If we divide parents into the musically-educated and those who don't know very much about music, the biggest problem for the first group is to inhibit the natural parental instinct to pass on their own prejudices and biases to the next generation. Generally, teachers are better at controlling this instinct because they are professionally aware of the dangers.

I often meet orchestral musicians who deplore their own children's interest in pop or jazz. When, for example, I suggest to a classically-orientated parent that a twelve-year-old who is bored with the piano and refuses to practise might be happier trying out an electric piano or organ or synthesiser, I get a look which implies that I had suggested abolishing every orchestra and assassinating Beethoven, Bach and the rest!

This is not a one-way problem. Parents who are obsessed with jazz or dance music or big bands should make it equally possible for their children to experience other kinds of music.

It's no justification for a parent to pass on his own bias by saying: "We weren't given any choice, in my day." In "our day" there may not have been much choice to make, for the proliferation of musical forms is a recent phenomenon and one which now makes the catholicity of opportunity for children pressing and so worth while.

Parents who go to concerts themselves want to take their children with them as soon as they are old enough. In assessing when a child is old enough to listen to the sophisticated complex of sound produced by a symphony orchestra, most concert-goers err on the young side. Children can't begin to appreciate a composite sound until they have first been taught how it is made up. Orchestras and orchestral concerts are no good for this.

Taking a young child to a symphony concert or most other adult concerts is akin to taking him to a Strindberg play or giving him a copy of *Crime and Punishment* to read. I'm sure there are a few children

Atarah and one of the musical animals at an Atarah's Band concert

who wallow in Strindberg, Dostoievsky and Shostakovich while their peers are still grappling with the mysteries of joined-up writing, but this book is not about them.

Parents who may themselves habitually travel long distances for their cultural pleasures will see nothing unusual in the idea of taking their children to the nearest big town for a specially-advertised "Children's concert", with a programme chosen for, and hopefully explained to, the children in the audience. But parents who do not go to the theatre or art exhibitions may simply not think of doing this.

Yet, at this stage, there is probably no effort which a parent can make which is more worth while, than that which is necessary to give the child the experience of *live* music.

Unhappily, there are very few properly planned, presented and performed children's concerts in Britain. It still distresses me that while so many adult musicians deplore the Great Cultural Divide, so few of them are prepared to start building bridges. It's much easier to churn out another performance of *Peter and the Wolf* and *The Carnival of Animals* . . .

A good compromise introduction to live music is to take a child to situations where musicians work incidentally, and preferably in small numbers so that the sound is not too "thick": to the theatre, pantomimes, summer shows, ballet, and even opera. This enables the child to concentrate primarily on the visual or dramatic activities on stage and gradually become aware of the music and how it is contributing to the overall experience.

Every parent begins naturally by looking after his or her own children, but there is no harm in using the same amount of effort to do some good for other people's children as well. If you live in an area where there are few or no live musical experiences available for your children, remember that they are not alone in this deprivation.

Complain!

Complain to your Regional Arts Association, to the Leisure Service Department of your local council, to your M.P., to the Arts Council of Great Britain (who'll try and shift the blame back to the R.A.A., but don't let them). All of these people have a duty (which you pay them to fulfil) to provide leisure facilities, and it is a duty which is – outside the major cities in Britain – appallingly badly executed. It is no excuse for them to tell you that the last time there was live music, the audience was bad. The audience for anything is bad if there is no pattern of regular availability. Even the attendance at Bingo would be bad if there was only one session a year and that wasn't very well advertised! If you get no satisfaction, write to the newspapers and don't give up.

If as little were done for football as is done for music in most local government areas of Britain, the result would be a turf-less square yard of mud with half a goal-post for all the local teams to play on. That analogy is a little too favourable to football because most rate-payers have stopped playing – or even watching – local games by their thirtieth birthday. Most people who enjoy music, do so throughout their lives.

Parents who live in areas lacking much professional music-making should not overlook the usefulness of amateur music as a source of inspiration for their children. There is today a resurgence of amateur music: of amateur orchestras, amateur operatic societies, bands, and choirs, all of which give public performances.

It is a cliché in the entertainment business that the audiences for these events are won more by arm-twisting than by advertisement, but they are generally good. It is far more stimulating for a child to begin his experience of live music by going to a well-attended amateur performance of *The Mikado*, perhaps knowing some of the people in the cast and some of the orchestra, than to be dragged off to some anonymous hall where an anonymous orchestra is playing anonymous (to the children) music. Many organisers of amateur events are keenly interested in encouraging children's interest, for obvious reasons.

It's important to see and hear the musical possibilities, which may lie within the family's financial and geographical reach, through the eyes and ears of the children. For many youngsters, there is far more inspiration to be had from the school end-of-term concert than from a brilliant performance by a great orchestra under a world-famous conductor. Hero-worshipping of older children playing in the school orchestra or jealousy of a friend who plays a couple of simple pieces in front of the class can provide much motivation!

Parents who live out of reach of the nearest concert hall make up the majority of our population. Yet they too can find live music if they know where to look. Certain parts of the country have their own special traditions, like the brass band cult of the North. Irish clubs with young children playing astonishingly well on penny-whistles and button accordions welcome visitors. Folk clubs and jazz clubs welcome and depend on a constant flow of young "fans".

The local junior brass band, Boy Scouts' band, Sea Cadets or CCF band, etc. make music relevant and accessible to children. It is thought-provoking that the bandmasters usually have had little musical training and thus keep all instruction and choice of arrangements, etc. on a very rudimentary level which all can cope with. They deserve medals.

A musically-educated parent can give much to a child in terms of communicating the joy of music so long as he doesn't seek to pass on prejudice and bias; exploring new fields of music with your children can actually be fun for you, too. I didn't discover folk music until after my thirtieth birthday, and rock even later ...

Remember that musically-educated parents have an easier job than those who think they "know nothing about music". Each week at the Children's Concert Centre I get many letters from the latter, asking for help and advice. I try to reply along these lines:

Dear Parent,

Firstly, you may be doing yourself an injustice. Most adults listen to some kind of music for pleasure, whether it's Andy Williams or Shirley Bassey or what happens to be on Radio One. It's quite possible to talk with your children about this kind of music and get them to make conscious choices between one group and another, between one song and another, between one version of a song and another version of the same song. The purpose of this is to make your child consciously aware that he already gets pleasure on some level from music, that there are choices to make, that music can offer different things to different people. Children are people, too, you know.

Banging on toy drums, blowing toy recorders and bashing away at Grandma's piano are fun, and there is no harm in this so long as everybody is aware that it doesn't lead anywhere. The harm in this area is the shoddiness of most toy instruments, which are *un*musical and which contradict any instinctive musicality in the child. Only a very talented parent/teacher will be able to lead children on from this sort of game-playing to learning to play, because, as we shall see, there are important *conscious* decisions which the child first has to make.

Take advantage of amateur music-making, particularly rehearsal-time. Most laymen would not think of walking in – let alone taking a child in – to rehearsal time of the local amateur orchestra or brass band or operatic society. Nor would they think of taking little children into a Music Centre run by the education authority, just "to see what is going on". Yet, most of the people involved in running this kind of activity in the community *understand* how important it is for children to pursue an interest, however vague and childish, in music and they will normally be the last people to discourage this kind of exploratory visit.

One important advantage of taking a child to a rehearsal, rather than to the performance, is that, when the child has had enough, you can go! A lot of the harm done by taking young children to performances is that the interest of the first five or ten minutes wanes as concentration goes and the child is forced by convention to stay and be bored for the rest of the show.

If there's a band marching in a parade along the street, encourage your child to express an interest in one favourite instrument and find out about that one at the library. Reduce music always to the level at which the child can be active, so just tackle one instrument at a time. The idea of "musical instruments" is too complex for a small child, but the idea of "finding out about trumpets or drums" is exciting.

Music programmes on television can be exploited in the same way. Watch children's programmes with your child – both Top of the Pops and orchestras – and see which kind of music attracts *your* child most. This will give you a guide as to which kind of records to buy.

An astonishing number of modern children think that the music they hear on television, radio and records is made by machines. This may seem laughable to adults, but how can a child begin to think of the possibility of playing an instrument himself unless he is first aware that *people*, not machines, make music?

Buy your child his own *records and cassettes* if at all possible. A cassette-player to have in the bedroom is worth hundreds of records which have to be played by an adult, for fear of damaging the stylus. Most record shops can get all the children's records on the market.

Parents get depressed at the content and musical standards of most children's records available in the shops. They may not be very good, but they are still better than no records at all.

Over the years, I have had many arguments with people who run our major record companies. They always defend themselves by saying that they are in business for profit and the market for children's records is only one per cent of the whole record market, inferring that it is not worth their while spending much time or effort or intelligence chasing so small a margin. Perhaps quality would improve demand? They shrug their shoulders and point to the rows of Golden Discs on the wall . . .

This is such a pity, because if a fraction of the intelligence that is devoted to the marketing of a new pop group were applied to researching what young children need and can benefit from, we might see some really exciting and worthwhile records for children commercially available in the shops. And, who knows? They might even increase their percentage . . .

We decided at the Children's Concert Centre to do something about it. We got together a record producer, parents, teachers, child musicians and some of the composers and arrangers who have worked with us over the years producing material for the Atarah's Band concerts. The result was the formation of a new record label to extend the repertoire of recordings for children. Our records and cassettes include stories (with music specially written), clapping games, skipping songs, nursery rhymes, simple and clear arrangements of music in all styles from classical tunes to gentle rock and pop. They're never simply entertainment, because children want to be educated.

The reaction from parents, complaining only that the records get worn out from repeated playing, shows that we are on the right track.

If records and cassettes seem too expensive to buy, remember that every public library should be able to supply records on free loan. If your Library can't offer this service, apply pressure, and don't think you are alone.

Remember that your rates and taxes pay for the services of a lot of people who have been professionally trained as musicians: orchestral players, music teachers, music advisers, Arts Association Music Officers, Leisure Service Officers, Music Centre Organisers. These people are paid to be involved in the musical welfare of your child. In the last analysis, if your children don't grow up to want music among their leisure activities, all these folk will be out of a job.

And, don't forget the example of other children. If there's a boy or girl, locally, who you know is learning an instrument, don't be shy. Go and ask if your child can come and listen and hold the instrument and talk to the child who is learning for a few minutes. Both the child and the parents involved will probably welcome the chance to "show off" a bit.

All this takes time, but being a parent does take time. If you think that the result could be to give your child a lifelong hobby and interest, you'll agree with me that it's worth it.

What can non-specialist teachers do?

We also get a lot of mail from non-specialist teachers all over Britain and hundreds of them come up to me at Atarah's Band live concerts, asking what they can do to make music accessible and fun for their children.

They have a tremendous burden and responsibility for guiding and awakening children in the formative years. Our society is so exam-orientated that we tend to think that the only important teac'.ers are the ones in secondary school who "get the children through" their exams, forgetting that unless a child has been given the right start at infants' and junior school, the chances of his being able to exploit even good teaching at the secondary stage are much reduced. So it is with music, yet, too often, the school system gives little help or support to non-specialist teachers working in this area.

It is a normal part of their duties to take "Music Lessons", which usually consist of singing, playing with recorders, simple percussion, and maybe strumming guitars.

The problem is that music is a complicated and highly specialised subject and there is very little help available on how to spend the obligatory music lessons in a happy and fruitful way. The musical establishment ought to be bending over backwards to provide basic help and advice and a choice of musically valid and progressive classroom music courses for use at this level, remembering that most of the children only hear pop music at home.

Some teachers exploit children's familiarity with recorded music by making up their own *musical quizzes* for children, recording snippets of favourite television signature tunes, children's request records on the radio, and so on. It's surprising to many adults just how much music children can recognize. It is a good idea to mix music from all periods and fields up together so that the children begin by hearing a diversity of sounds. Given a choice of two or more pieces, always pick the one with the simpler arrangement; it's easier to listen to. When playing music to children even in the classroom bear in mind that the length of the average pop song is about two and a half minutes, for the very good reason that that is the longest any child can happily concentrate on music.

Often they encourage the children to write down or draw any story or picture suggested by familiar music, dramatic music, pompous music, and so on.

I'm always delighted when a teacher sends me compositions or drawings done by the children after a visit to Atarah's Band. Junior school teachers are generally good at organising this kind of thing, sending written and graphical material to orchestras, bands and other musicians the children may have contacted, but they can also organise the same sort of thing in reference to television programmes the children watch. Usually, the Production Office of the programme will reply – and, if the accompanying letter is cunningly worded, send some kind of "bonus" in return, such as a prize for the class or for the best entry.

Local Councils and Arts Associations would probably be delighted to display an exhibition of such children's work. Building societies and banks are always looking for bright and interesting material to put in the High Street windows and it is a great encouragement for children to see their own pictures and stories on public display.

Children like to make things, and making instruments is a splendid classroom activity. It's not so difficult as might be thought to make simple drums, xylophones from milk bottles and, of course, flutes, both blown into and blown across.

I started to play the flute as a direct result of playing the recorder and the reason why I took up the recorder in the first place is that a teacher organised my class to make instruments. I made a crude bamboo recorder which wasn't very good, for I was a clumsy child, yet the pleasure and sense of achievement of actually making an instrument that worked provided the impetus which eventually landed me on the concert platform.

All this talk of *activities* is deliberate. The least productive thing is to sit a class down and make it listen passively to music. The earlier the children connect the idea of music with doing something, the better.

Any of the projects which parents can do in the home will work better in the classroom because the impetus of a group of children working together can impel even the slowest child a lot further than it could travel alone.

Why not arrange more musical *events* for infant and junior school-children? Not visits to symphony orchestras which they're not equipped to understand, let alone enjoy, but simpler performances.

Every County or District Music Adviser can arrange visits by his peripatetic staff to come and play a little and talk a lot to the children. Because a "peripatetic" teaches instrumental technique to teenagers, this does not mean that he necessarily has any idea how to *inspire* six- or eight-year olds. The class teacher should remember that he or she is the expert in dealing with young children and not be afraid to act as the interpreter or – as on a television programme – the interviewer, asking the questions which will interest the children but which they may not be able to formulate themselves.

A simple, good format for this kind of "visit" is:

1 Introductory chat – brief!
2 Play – a little.
3 Explain.
4 Let children try an instrument for themselves.
5 Teacher's Question Time.
6 Children's Question Time.
7 Play a little.
8 Applause – the class should thank the "performer" for the "Show" they have enjoyed.

The performer's Golden Rule – in all work for children – is: You're not here for the pleasure of playing, but to work for your audience: the children.

In the same way that teacher-training colleges send student teachers into school for teaching practice, any Further Education institution which runs courses including music should send its students out into the junior schools to talk, particularly to the younger children, about the joys and realities of making music. The non-specialist teachers and head teachers who pressure for this kind of "event" for the children should aim at a comprehensive range of instruments (one after another, not all together) including guitars, drums and synthesisers as well as fiddles, woodwind and conventional percussion.

Whether or not it is possible to find a demonstrator/performer within the educational system, teachers can *easily* organize classroom concerts by local professional and semi-professional musicians. The cost of organising some musical events is surprisingly low and it may well be within the financial reach of several non-specialist teachers and their children – with or without assistance from school funds – to hire a local folk singer or rock group to come and play a little and talk a lot to the children. It's most effective if the audience is kept within a small age-range. This makes it easier for the performers to talk to the children and gives altogether greater impact to the whole "show". Follow-up work in writing and drawing and painting and acting can last a long time!

Performers/demonstrators don't have to be adult. Children get a lot from seeing and hearing coevals and older children from an associated school performing – even on simple instruments. Even very young children who can play should be encouraged to perform in front of the class and to talk about what is nice, and what is difficult, about the instrument in question, what their musical ambitions are, and so on . . .

When there is cost involved in setting up a classroom concert – or a visit to a musical event outside the school – nobody should feel shy about asking parents to pay for tickets. Most parents are delighted that the school is prepared to take the children out and happily pay a realistic price. Speaking from our own experience at the Children's Concert Centre which manages around 200 concerts every year – many of them for audiences of schoolchildren – the children get more from the experience for which they have paid than from a "free" one. This is doubtless a reflection of our materialistic age, but it is a fact.

I have deliberately left until last what might seem the most obvious way to spend music lessons: teaching the children to play recorders and simple percussion instruments, and to strum guitars and sing.

It's worth examining carefully the benefits which children can obtain from this kind of musical activity. From learning to play simple tunes on a recorder, they can acquire a basis for the future ability to read music, but the connection of a particular dot on a particular line of the stave with the fingering of a certain note on the recorder is not the same as the ability to "read music". It is the exact parallel of recognising letters, not reading words.

The recorder can be a wonderfully revealing instrument. It *can* expose a talent for music which is within a child. Learning to play simple tunes on the recorder and learning to play together with other children in recorder choirs can be a worthwhile experience in its own right. Similarly, percussion-playing can be a pleasant class activity, but neither recorder-playing, whether solo or in recorder choirs, nor percussion-playing *automatically* lead to any next stage.

Playing simple percussion instruments *can* reveal and extend the innate comprehension of rhythm which many children have; some of the percussion methods, of which the best known is Carl Orff's, can in themselves be a valid and pleasurable programme of activities, but there is a yawning gulf between the furthest point which most children under most non-specialist teachers will ever reach on the recorder or in percussion groups and the beginning of legitimate musical study.

This kind of fun music in the classroom makes music lessons very enjoyable – which is what music should be – but simple musical activities do not lead on to a worthwhile study of a truly musical subject or of instrumental technique. The business of "leading on" can only be handled by specialist teachers, who don't get involved with children under eleven except in areas where – usually as a direct result of the energy and resourcefulness of an individual Music Adviser – children have the opportunity to start music lessons under specialist teachers on more complicated instruments when they are ready.

Strumming guitars also passes a few music lessons quite pleasantly. Children like the idea of being able to accompany their own voices. But learning a few unrelated chords does not lead anywhere on an instrument as difficult as the guitar. Children can often be left feeling very frustrated when the teacher runs out of chords and there is "nowhere to go".

The gist of my advice to non-specialist teachers – unless they happen to have had a musical training – is to regard music lessons as fun-with-music and not as direct preparation.

What can specialist teachers do?

Specialist music teachers who teach privately concentrate upon individual children and specific areas of technique. Specialist teachers in schools come in two kinds: the in-school music teachers and the peripatetic teachers who are deployed by the Music Adviser to teach instrumental technique in a number of schools.

The business of inspiring children of secondary school age rests largely with the in-school music teacher. He has a variety of roles to play: in some cases he will be nurturing and extending the inspiration of home, of the media, of previous NST influence; he has constantly to be vigilant to find the right keys and the right moment to "turn" individual children towards music and learning an instrument; he has to develop a genius for making the ultra-abstract subject of theory into something useful and exciting; he has to come to terms, without being defeatist, with the inevitability of most children opting out of music lessons after two or three years, yet utilise the time for which they are with him to give them as wide and exciting an experience of music as possible.

The last task is far more difficult than it might seem. The music teacher will usually be classically-trained and classically-orientated. Most of his pupils are "heavily into pop".

He has to remember that he is an ambassador from the world of music as far as the children are concerned. If he shows himself as a restricted *aficionado* of one particular kind of music or one particular family of instruments, he can do more than anyone else to alienate children from music. After all, children are no more stupid than adults and if the first musician they meet (the specialist teacher) does not communicate that music is a source of fun and joy, but rather a sterile and mutually painful way of spending a few boring lessons, they will draw their own conclusions.

Section 4
The Decision to Learn

What happens next after a child has been inspired to an interest in music?

Some children – a minority – will want to reflect their personalities by exercising a passive interest in music. They will start to collect records, read books about musicians, pay more attention to television and radio programmes about the kind of music which they like.

However, the nature of childhood is not passive. The majority of children will want to pursue their new interest actively. They will want to make music. Many will be attracted to the idea of making vocal music, but most children will pursue an active interest by wanting to make music on an instrument. Because instruments are machines, they offer – and even a child is capable of appreciating this – far more exciting possibilities of making music than the human voice can extend to.

Children are familiar with the idea of learning to operate a machine. They find nothing strange about this, whether the machine is a television set, a bicycle, a supermarket trolley, or a lift. They are quite capable of seeing a musical instrument as a (subtle and complicated) machine. They are not surprised by the implication that it will take more time and application to master an instrument than a bicycle.

The vital stage which must follow upon inspiration if the child is to make real progress in music is that the child has to make a *conscious decision to learn* the instrument.

There is no reason to hide from any child that learning an instrument is hard work. Children come to know the difference between play and work, at school. They are quite able to decide to work at something which interests them.

However, a conscious decision to learn is beyond the capacity of most pre-school children, or those in the very early stages at infant school. They have not first learned the difference between play and work.

It is impossible to over-emphasize the importance of this conscious decision. A child who is persuaded by parents to have lessons on the piano has not made a conscious decision and will almost certainly founder for no other reason, irrespective of whatever musical potential he may have. A child who is persuaded by well-meaning parents that innocently *playing with* instruments, e.g. messing about with a few chords on the guitar, will lead automatically to being able to play properly and make music – is being cheated by the parents. They are, in effect, denying the child the opportunity of making the necessary conscious decision.

Parents and teachers often consult me about the vast numbers of children who apparently do well on simple percussion instruments or playing tunes on the recorder, and yet "fail" on transferring to a more complicated instrument which requires a sustained course of study. The answer is simply that the children have not made a conscious decision to learn. As soon as they find out that they have been tricked and that this isn't just another musical game, they understandably get disheartened and give up.

It is quite possible for a very dominant parent to "push" a child in many activities including music. Such domination may replace the child's own decision-making apparatus and if the domination continues, the child may make excellent progress, driven by the will-power of the parent. "Excellent progress" means here passing the exams without problem, practising to order, yet failing to fulfil the child's own musical needs.

If the parent loses interest, or, as is more likely, the child comes to assert his own personality and combats the parental domination, this will usually lead to a "failure" on the musical side, because there was no initial conscious decision on the part of the child.

By making this decision, the child has already foregone any simple dream of picking up the instrument and making music straight away. He has put over the immediate horizon the eventual attainment of fluency on the instrument and accepted the more immediate challenges.

"Practising is all right . . . when you start to learn the piano, you know it's going to be hard work." (Susannah, age 10: Grade 1 piano)

"There were six of us started flute lessons when they said we could have them free, from this teacher who came to the school.

"I think some of the other girls only came to get out of R.E. . . . You didn't have to pay for the instruments, either. All the others dropped out after the first term, when it got hard. I think they thought it was going to be easy." (Janet, aged 12: Grade 3 flute)

One of the many paradoxes of music is that one can only realise the wonderful dream of making music by going through the protracted slog of learning an instrument. Children are capable of making decisions of this nature and it is the duty of adults who are associated with this stage in a child's approach to music to help the child to be honest about his attitude.

Children know that learning involves hard work and are capable of making the decision to learn

Section 5
Matching the Child and the Instrument

Choosing an instrument – the negative way

I was in a music shop browsing through sheet music and checking prices of instruments for a radio programme when a girl of eleven came in with her mother to buy an instrument. Literally: "to buy an instrument". They had come to the shop because the girl wanted to play *something*. At the moment of coming through the shop door they had no firm intention of buying any particular instrument but simply of getting something which the girl could learn without too many problems. She had shown what the parents and her non-specialist teacher thought was a good deal of progress on the recorder and therefore her vague preference was for a woodwind instrument, probably a flute or a clarinet.

They asked the advice of the shop assistant who suggested the girl should try a flute and a clarinet and say which one felt better. She tried both instruments and managed to get one or two notes out of each and was then left helpless to make a decision.

Once this particular family had spent £70 on an instrument, they were very unlikely to trade it in and buy another, so the decision was going to have a lasting effect.

Because the girl couldn't make up her mind, her mother suggested that she had made a nicer sound on the flute and that they ought to buy that. The girl thought for a moment and said that she didn't like being unable to see her fingers on the flute and that she thought the clarinet suited her more because she could look down the line of the instrument, see her fingering and see the music in front of her all the time – just as on the recorder. Also she had found it "less hard work" to produce a sound on the clarinet.

When I could no longer stand the tension, I introduced myself and asked if I could help. It took a few seconds only because the girl had prominent upper front teeth which are well suited to the clarinet and completely unsuited to the flute. Also, she was physically rather frail and did not, in my opinion, have the sheer "guts" to push the air over the open hole of a flute. Given the overall preference for a flute or clarinet, there was no doubt in my mind that she would never make a good flute player but she could make a good clarinettist.

To put it in another way, it was unlikely she would ever get much *pleasure* from playing the flute and very likely that she would get a lot of joy from learning the clarinet.

An oboist friend of mine confessed, after years of playing with me in an orchestra, that she'd never wanted to play the oboe and had always wanted to play the flute! When she was twelve, the school had had a spare oboe but nobody had had either the money or a spare instrument to give her a flute. Out of the cupboard came the oboe and because she had a great deal of natural musical talent, she progressed through all the stages to become a professional oboist, unhappy with her instrument from start to finish and never having the courage to write off all the effort that had gone into learning the wrong instrument, and change to the right one.

As a third example, a very sensitive and keenly intelligent composer confided in me that his initial musical training had been on the trombone, which he found a very frustrating and unsatisfactory instrument. At the age of twelve, he'd asked the music teacher at school to be allowed to learn an instrument – any instrument. The teacher had failed to take into account the lad's mental and emotional needs and simply said: "Well, you've got long arms, you do the trombone".

From talking with other musicians and from meeting children at all stages of learning, I could cite hundreds of different examples of this casual mis-matching of children with instruments which do not suit them mentally or emotionally or physically.

Sometimes it is impossible for a family to afford the right instrument for a child. Bassoons and French horns are simply too expensive for most households to obtain. Yet, the majority of cases of mis-matching which I come across are due to two reasons: ignorance and laziness.

By spending a proper degree of intelligence and a reasonable amount of time, it is possible to match any child with the right instrument on which he is most likely to succeed. This is the positive way of choosing an instrument.

Choosing an instrument – the positive way

Non-musicians often fail to appreciate the difference in physical and mental attributes called for by different instruments.

Anybody advising a child or helping a child to arrive at his own decision about taking up a specific instrument should try to avoid pre-conceptions or bias and forget what might be useful to the school, or what the family tradition was, or how easy it is to obtain a particular instrument, and assess the child clinically – in a kind of musical diagnosis.

I spend a lot of time with my own mature students, particularly those who are going into in-school and peripatetic teaching, helping them to develop their own instinct for this area of our work.

Natural teachers have an instinct which often tells them what is right for a child. They can sense when a child is physically and mentally at ease in a particular situation, or when the child is not comfortable. They can sense when a child is in contact with a subject and when he is just learning by rote. They can sense the difference between a child who is trying hard at the wrong subject and one who is "at home" in the subject.

However, even without much instinctive feeling for what is going on in a child's mind, it is possible to make a number of detailed observations which tell you:

> whether the child is physically comfortable on the instrument;
>
> whether he is robust enough for the work of blowing, hitting, or scraping required by the instrument;
>
> whether he is big enough to operate the instrument without straining;
>
> whether he has the mental capacity to play the kind of music which is written for the instrument;
>
> whether the temperament of the child suits the instrument;
>
> whether he has the emotional need to be with others or prefers to be on his own.

By thus breaking down the complex of questions to be answered in the process of matching the child with the right instrument, it is possible to see that many of the questions are not in themselves difficult for even a non-musician to work out.

The Bentovim Children's Music Centre is the only body organised to help in this process: we have a complete range of instruments for the child to try, which covers most conceivable choices. We literally move from the Woodwind Room to the String Room to the Rock Studio to the Percussion Room to the Brass Room, if need be, in our search for the right instrument for any one child. Whilst this isn't possible at home and may not be possible even in most schools, anyone can take a child into a large music shop and do more or less the same thing. No sensible salesman minds spending half an hour letting a child try lots of instruments.

Given this choice of instruments, many children simply *know* when they pick up the right one. For those who are not a hundred per cent certain, there are a number of useful guidelines.

The positive way – woodwind

With the exception of the oboe, woodwind instruments are excellent for children who need quick and early satisfactions. Because each note is produced by a specific fingering, there's no question of having to pitch individual notes. Flute and bassoon are almost a push-over for children who have learnt the recorder. Provided the child has the right-shaped mouth (lips and teeth) for the instrument chosen, it's possible to make a satisfying sound from the beginning and to play simple tunes within a few weeks.

The physical work of blowing a woodwind instrument should not be overlooked. I am personally against children seriously beginning a wind instrument before the age of ten. The clarinet, and surprisingly the bassoon, require the least physical effort. To play the flute requires enormous hard work from the belly muscles to force a constant volume of air across the open hole of the flute. This often makes children dizzy (indeed it can make professional flautists feel as though they're drunk after a heavy concert!).

Because so many children first play the recorder, all too often parents and teachers assume that they should progress to another woodwind instrument. This wrong assumption has produced large numbers of frustrated flute-players and clarinettists who would have been much happier on strings or brass.

The flute

The flute requires teeth which are not large and lips which are not too full. I've never known a child with a lisp able to play the flute because the tongueing is done *within* the mouth (there is no reed). Children with small hands may find the span required to play the flute painful, in which case I don't recommend deliberately stretching the hand. The piccolo which is basically a scaled-down flute is physically within their grasp, but it is a much harder instrument to play and not one on which I would start a child younger than twelve because the internal abdominal and inter-cranial pressure generated by blowing the piccolo are quite considerable.

The flute suits quick-thinking children who can't be bothered to plug away at dull basic chores. It's possible to move very fast on the flute and be playing tunes within a few weeks and taking part in a junior orchestra within six months. Quick initial progress does not mean that you have a prodigy on your hands! The flute is a good choice for sociable children, because whilst the solo repertoire is a bit thin on the ground, there is a lifetime of music to play with piano, in small groups and in orchestras.

The mechanics of the flute are simpler than those of any other woodwind instrument, which makes second-hand flutes a good buy, so long as they have been reasonably well looked after or well overhauled.

The oboe

The oboe suits children with thin lips or tight mouths because the lips have to be folded back over the teeth in order to grip the reed and produce the sound. The characteristic disadvantage of the oboe is that so little air can be forced through the reed. This builds up a colossal pressure in the upper chest cavity and, indeed, in the blood vessels of the head, which makes me very wary of letting young children begin this instrument. (Many professional oboe players have permanent haemorrhage of facial blood vessels and indeed there is some body of thought that emphysema is virtually a professional hazard.)

To produce a pleasant sound on the oboe is far more difficult than on any other woodwind instrument. In junior orchestras, they tease the oboist by saying that he sounds like a duck quacking the whole time; nor is it a coincidence that Prokofiev gave the Duck's tune in *Peter and the Wolf* to the oboe!

Developing and controlling the muscles of the embouchure for the oboe takes a long time and is a nerve-racking process, discouraging for children who lack a lot of patience and the necessary obsession. Children who succeed with the oboe have often had previous experience on another instrument, to get some of the "basics" out of the way before tackling the problems peculiar to this instrument.

Many children are drawn to the oboe because it undoubtedly has within its repertoire some of the most beautiful tunes in orchestral music, but, unless a child is certain about wanting to play the oboe, it is not an instrument I would recommend.

The basic design of the flute and clarinet has changed little of recent years, but the oboe is still a developing instrument. It is inadvisable to buy one before finding a teacher and getting his advice. There are several different systems of fingering, and many oboes at the cheaper end of the market (and even some bought for high sums by professional oboists) can be forever unsatisfactory to play. I know few contented oboists! But, again, a neurotic child who needs an excuse to worry, could find the oboe a good therapy. (Finding or making reeds, alone, can be a full-time occupation!)

The clarinet

The B flat clarinet is probably the easiest instrument and, at the early stages, the most satisfying of the whole woodwind family. Good strong front teeth, but not necessarily protruding ones, are a help for playing the clarinet. There are plenty of children who cannot get a note out of the flute, but I've yet to come across a child who can't

obtain the small but important satisfaction of getting a note from a clarinet at the first attempt, simply because the mechanics of the reed assist so much in the production of the sound. The disadvantage of the reed is that it can be a bit of a strain on pocket money, because the more you practise, the quicker even good reeds will wear out and need replacement – and they're not cheap.

Children who have become reasonably fluent on recorder find no problems fingering flute, piccolo, oboe, bassoon or saxophone because the basic system is the same: to change the octave, you just blow harder.

Transferring from recorder to clarinet is a much bigger step. The fingering is radically different, because the clarinet "overblows a twelfth"; in other words, if you blow harder, you go up not one octave but an octave and a half. Thus the same note in different octaves has a different fingering. Surprisingly, children adjust to this technique more easily than adults.

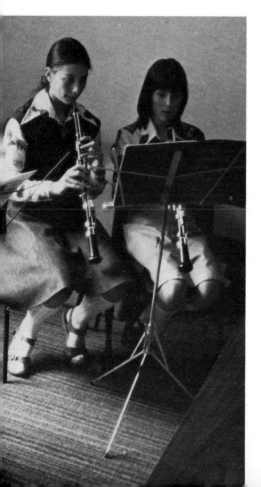

The positive way – woodwind. Instruments left to right: clarinet, flute, oboes

Because the clarinet was a late-comer on the classical scene, it has intrigued many composers to write for it, with a resultant extensive repertoire of music to play, exploiting the enormous range of notes which it can reach.

It's an exciting instrument to play. Whilst it has no great solo repertoire, it suits outgoing children who want to play in groups, whether in classically-orientated orchestras or in the freer jazz and

14-year-old bassoonist

improvising situations. A good clarinet to learn on need not be too expensive.

The bassoon

The bassoon is a big instrument which suits relatively large children. The span required for fingering the keys is considerable. Smaller children will find it an agony, even with the bassoon supported on a spike or a sling, to stretch from the position of the right-hand little finger on the bottom key to the mouth on the mouthpiece. Despite the size of the instrument, it does not take a great deal of energy to blow.

Many bassoon pupils are "plodders" who are happy to make what appears to be slow progress, and have an appreciation of the bass sound and harmony rather than always wanting to play tunes. An extrovert "show-off" would be miserable on the bassoon.

The bassoon is an excellent instrument for children of thirteen or fourteen who already play the piano or some other instrument and want to take up a second study.

The peripheral advantage of playing the bassoon is that it's relatively easy to get into youth orchestras and university and college orchestras because there's far less competition on this instrument than on the rest of the woodwind family.

A crippling disadvantage for many families who haven't outside finance available is that bassoons are four or five times as expensive as flutes or clarinets and two or three times as expensive as oboes.

The recorder

The recorder is a serious instrument in its own right, but it is also an excellent first instrument and very useful for assessing general musical ability in children.

Once a child starts to play "real music" on the recorder, technique becomes extremely difficult. The instrument itself is so simple that many notes have to be played by cross-fingering. (It was to overcome the contortions of this, that the elaborate key-work of the later woodwind instruments was evolved).

Although there is much early music and Baroque music playable on the recorder, which can be a great joy to children who respond to the special charm of that music, it is a frustrating instrument for children who want to play music of other styles or periods.

Although apparently simple to look at, good instruments (bass, tenor, treble and descant recorders) are not cheap.

The alto saxophone

The alto saxophone is a casual visitor to the woodwind section of the orchestra, and far more at home in jazz bands, dance bands and pop music. Because of this it is underestimated as an instrument for children. Classical bias, again!

It is basically easy to play; quality of sound is the only area of technique which requires prolonged hard work.

The sax is a true hybrid: made of brass, but belonging with the woodwind; fingered like a flute, but blown with a reed, like the clarinet.

The repertoire is limited, since the sax was only invented in 1890, but for a child who wants to make rapid progress and isn't much interested in classical music, this can be an excellent choice.

Doubling instruments

These are the "second" instruments played by musicians. Few children will get involved with them, but the doubling instruments in the woodwind family are:

First instrument	Doubling instruments
flute	piccolo, alto flute
oboe	cor anglais
B flat clarinet	clarinets in E flat and A, bass clarinet
bassoon	contra-bassoon
alto saxophone	tenor sax and baritone sax

The positive way – strings

All the instruments in the strings section of an orchestra are really fiddles of different sizes. Because the fiddle is such a simple machine, it places great demands on the player. Each note has to be pitched by ear, every time it is played, without the technical assistance of keys, valves or frets.

To make any progress on a string instrument, most children will need much help and encouragement in the home, as well as regular lessons. This family of instruments is without doubt the most demanding, which is why strings are generally played well only by intelligent, sensitive people!

Because fiddles can play fast and high, laymen think that they call for a bright and lively intelligence, yet the successful junior string player is more likely to be a conscientious plodder than a quick-witted extrovert. The child who can progress to playing happy tunes on the flute or clarinet after six weeks' learning will take at least a year to achieve the same fluency on the fiddle.

The violin

The violin is the undoubted king of instruments. Like a true king, it demands the most and is undeniably the richest. At the same time, it is perhaps the most abused instrument in schools, simply because it is easy to buy mass-produced cheap violins. (It's perhaps not an easy choice to decide whether, from a limited budget, to buy one flute or clarinet, or three cheap violins.) Yet for every hundred children who can find a great deal of pleasure and satisfaction on the clarinet or flute or trumpet, you'd be lucky to find more than two or three who can get anything from the violin, particularly starting on an unpromising cheap instrument in a class situation – except, perhaps, in the rare situation where the Suzuki method is employed.

It's a pity that so many children are started on the violin at school for financial reasons, and because the half-size instruments can be held and played by small children. Nobody should think that this is an easy instrument. Everything about it, about its playing, about the sound, about its repertoire, about the kind of people that violinists are, screams at us from the outset that this is an instrument to be treated with considerable care. It is perhaps the greatest discourager of all instruments.

To be suited to the violin, a child must be intelligent, patient, conscientious and self-sufficient – content to practise and play on his own for a long time before getting together with others. This is an instrument which suits the "loner", not the outgoing child. Even in school orchestras, violin players tend to be pretty unsociable, because they have so many preoccupations with their instruments and their parts which are the most difficult of all the string sections.

The relationship with the teacher is even more important for a child learning the violin than any other instrument. It will be a long time until the child can produce a pleasant sound and during the long uphill struggle (it may well take two or three years' hard work to get to Grade 1) the child will depend for morale upon the contact with both teacher and parents. The Suzuki method places a great emphasis upon parental "participation".

Against all these problems, children who don't get discouraged in the early stages can go on to find this instrument a great boon in later life – whether on their own or in amateur chamber music groups or orchestras. No violinist will ever exhaust the repertoire of pleasurable and worthwhile music for his instrument.

The viola

The viola is sometimes wrongly thought of as just a big violin, but it is an instrument in its own right, both physically and musically. Because of its range, the viola has its own clef to prove the case for a separate identity. Learning to read viola (alto) clef is a little odd at first, but children adjust to it easily.

Children usually take up the viola at the age of ten or eleven, when their bodies – and particularly their arms – are large enough to cope with the size of the instrument. It is possible to begin earlier on a viola-strung violin or a three-quarter-size viola.

Frequently, children who have begun to learn the violin, but find they don't have the necessary mental or physical make-up for the true fiddle, change to the viola and find a peace and serenity in playing this instrument which more than compensates for its lack of repertoire and brilliance. Leaving aside the occasional jazz or folk use of the instrument, the viola is inhibiting because it inclines only towards classical music in orchestras and chamber ensembles.

In case that makes it sound like an instrument for plodders, I should point out that the viola requires perhaps a more measured intelligence than the violin, an equal sensitivity and an excellent ear because the viola player is not chugging away at the bottom, where the bass is, nor is he playing the top line of the tune. In order to play the middle part, he has to be right with both the violin on top and the 'cello below.

Many viola players have a melancholy about them which one can find echoed in the sound of their beautiful instrument. I'm not sure whether the frustration of having to do all the work of a violinist for so little obvious reward is responsible, or whether it is the temperament which dictates taking up the instrument in the first place. Most of the good viola players I've ever known have been delightful, sensitive, intelligent people. I only wish, for their own sake, that they could be described as happy. They're not the sort of people you'd ask along to cheer up a party!

The 'cello

The 'cello rarely comes to mind as an instrument for children, but it has a lot to recommend it. It is so much easier to get a pleasant sound from a 'cello than from a violin, on which the beginner's efforts can be aural agony, both for himself and also for all those within earshot! It was the fifth instrument which I studied and I was surprised how far it was possible to get in a short space of time and how much pleasure there was in playing the 'cello, both alone and in orchestras and simple string quartets.

The influx of cheap foreign instruments, particularly from Japan and China, is causing a reappraisal of the 'cello because it is now possible to buy one for the same price as a flute or clarinet.

'Cellos come in half and three-quarter sizes which avoids the physical problem of matching body size to instrument. *If* you can find an instrument of the right size, seven or eight is a good age at which to begin. A child of this age who is desperate to learn an instrument and doesn't favour the piano (or whose house cannot accommodate one!) should certainly think about taking up the 'cello, which is an instrument to start young, so that the left hand comes easily to form the postures required when playing.

The 'cello can give a lifetime's pleasure. It has a rich repertoire in classical music. There are never enough 'cellists of whatever standard,

Viola players in school orchestra

which makes one very popular both for orchestral and chamber music.

Even the beginner's repertoire is not discouraging. There are plenty of simple tunes. A particular delight of the 'cello is that it has a solo repertoire of its own as well as the bass or continuo role. There are few extrovert 'cellists – they tend to be conscientious, methodical people. Physically, the instrument probably suits girls even better than boys. Children who play it get great joy from what I can only call the mental and physical "solidarity" peculiar to this instrument.

The double-bass

The double-bass has one big disadvantage for children – its size! Yet, for a child big enough to handle it, it can be the most versatile of the stringed instruments: equally at home in the sociable bass section of a symphony orchestra, or "playing solo" in the rhythm section of dance and jazz bands.

A lot of the time, the double-bass is used simply for its bass effect, like the tuba going "oompah". Children who are "into pop" will be more interested in the louder, faster electric bass guitar.

As so often with bass instruments, scarcity makes a good double-bass player welcome everywhere.

Given physical size and strength, particularly in the left hand, it is fairly easy to make a good deal of progress within the limitations of the instrument and repertoire, but tunes are few and far between, which makes this an instrument unsuited to the dominant extrovert. It does suit the sociable child who is exact, conscientious and happy to stay in the background. Because of their size and the problem of transporting them, good instruments, even for a beginner, are hard to find and may have been damaged.

The positive way – brass

All instruments are machines to produce musical sound. Some very complicated machines like pianos go so far as to actually make the desired notes simply by the operator pressing a different key for each note. Woodwind instruments are medium-complicated: with the keys in any one position, there is a small choice of notes which can be produced, depending upon the amount of "puff".

Brass instruments are very simple machines: basically just a mouthpiece against which the lips are vibrated (as in blowing a raspberry), connected to a long piece of tubing with a bell at the other end. Far from having one key for each note, the trumpet, for example, has a range of two and a half octaves and only three valves. The player has to develop a special embouchure or attitude of lips to the mouthpiece. By adjusting this embouchure and without touching the keys, pistons or slide, he can achieve a range of notes. Since he cannot say: "I'm pressing down that key, therefore the note I'm playing is C" (for example), he has to train his ear far more rigorously than any woodwind player, or pianist.

In some areas of Britain, particularly the North, there is a traditional and family leaning towards the brass instruments. Where there are youth sections of brass bands, Boy Scout and Boys' Brigade bands and the like, the motivation may be very strong for children to take up brass instruments to join in and play with their friends. This peer-approval can be very important in supporting a child's early efforts.

I spent so many years in orchestras that I was unable not to come to some conclusions about the character of the musicians who play the various families of instruments. It is nearly always the case that brass players are extrovert, easy-going people – ideal to make up a football team or organise the orchestra's children's party. They are the first into the pub at the end of rehearsal (with the ludicrous excuse that they are "thirstier" than the rest of us!). They tend to be people with a lot of physical energy.

The trumpet

The trumpet is a very powerful top-line instrument. It can't be a coincidence that so many band leaders and other extrovert musical celebrities have been trumpeters. The instrument seems to suit the more outgoing, less introspective personality. The cliché close-up of a trumpet player shows the air pressure distending the cheeks, the veins distended in the forehead, sweat pouring off from sheer physical tension and exertion. Despite the advances of Women's Lib – even within the Musicians' Union – there are relatively few female trumpeters.

It takes a great deal of energy to blow hard or high, so the trumpet is not an instrument which I recommend for children younger than ten or eleven years old. Many adult brass players have badly deformed teeth and gums as a result of starting to play their instruments too young, before the gums are firm.

A sense of pitch is far more important than a quick brain.

The trumpet is an excellent instrument for sociable children – there is such a wealth of music written for the trumpet in military bands, brass bands and dance bands that it suits children who have no family or other inclination towards classical music.

With the right-shaped mouth and a reasonably good ear, children can make rapid progress on the trumpet, especially with the incentive of playing in a junior band.

The cornet

The cornet demands less physical effort and, although often thought of as the introductory instrument for children to start on until they are old enough to play a trumpet, it is – in the brass band world – very much an instrument in its own right. The Solo Cornet in a brass band is regarded much like the Leader in a symphony orchestra.

It is usual to start the cornet at eight or nine, playing very simple parts in brass band arrangements.

The trombone

The trombone is – like the viola in the String section – an often overlooked, quiet, but vital contributor to all kinds of music. The trombonist has the advantage that he is equally at home in a symphony orchestra, a jazz band, or a dance band. The most obvious candidates for the trombone are quiet, sensitive children of about thirteen or fourteen sufficiently tall to cope with the physical demands of the slide. Because the trombone rarely plays the tune, the trombonist is required to have an even better sense of pitch than the trumpet player. Girls often seem to do well on this instrument.

A quiet and undemanding intelligence tends to go with the trombone. The trombonist usually has a responsive role, with the more dominant trumpet playing the top line.

The trombone is an excellent instrument for a second study.

The French horn

The French horn is a nightmare. Indeed, it's the closest thing to a boa constrictor in the entire orchestra – twenty–two feet of brass plumbing with which to fight for every note and only four rotary valves to help you.

A lot of professional players have nervous breakdowns because the problem of pitching on this instrument means that even the established professional can never afford to relax for a moment. It needs an exceptionally good ear.

I doubt whether many people have got far on the French horn without previous musical experience.

The brass section of Manchester North Music Centre Concert Band,
recording for Piccadilly Radio's "Atarah's Music Box" series.
Top to bottom: trumpets, French horns

To learn to read music, begin musical theory and simultaneously tackle the French horn without prior instrumental experience is more than most people can take on. Moreover, the physical pressure involved puts it out of the question for younger children if we consider their general health and physique more important than learning an instrument – which I do.

Although sometimes found in bands and brass and wind ensembles, the French horn is more at home in symphony orchestras. It suits the obsessive genuine introvert who's prepared to give up a great deal for the joy of those rare moments when he is rewarded by the wonderful purity of tone which only this instrument can ever produce.

French horns – even second-hand – are seldom cheap and, like all brass instruments, are best bought with a teacher's advice.

The tuba

Because it looks the typical "oompah-oompah" instrument, the tuba is often treated – by composers, among others – as the chubby little clown of the orchestra. Despite its apparent bulk, it is surprisingly easy to blow, taking only a fraction of the effort required by the flute.

It's not derogatory to say that tuba parts are usually intellectually and musically undemanding but most enjoyable to play. No band is complete without a tuba and since too many children are attracted by the glamour of the higher brass instruments, any reasonably good player on the lower-pitched brass will find himself in demand.

Other brass instruments

The other brass instruments have many similarities with the above, since all brass instruments are variations on the basic bugle concept and design. Here are a few useful notes about them:

The bugle is the Brass equivalent of the recorder, a very good introductory instrument but also good fun to play in its own right, particularly in marching bands or by children with ambitions to go into the Forces.

The Flugelhorn is really a big cornet but, because of its characteristic rich tone, is much used in jazz writing and improvising. It is usually played by trumpeters as their main doubling instrument, and in brass bands.

Above: Tenor horns

Below: Euphonium

The tenor horn and baritone horn	are brass band instruments which are easy to blow and have undemanding parts. Light to carry and hold, they seem to be growing in favour with girls.
	Although they look large for young children to hold, they require surprisingly little physical effort to blow.
The euphonium	is the solo bass instrument of the brass band. Not a "funny" bass instrument, it has a moving pathos all of its own.

The doubling instruments in the brass section are:

Piccolo trumpet, D trumpet	
C trumpet, and posthorn	for the trumpeter;
Bass trombone	for the trombonist

The positive way – percussion

There are two families of percussion instruments: the tuned and the untuned.

UNTUNED PERCUSSION

The untuned percussion is made up of all the instruments which can be hit or shaken but which cannot be tuned. That is to say that it is not possible for the player to vary (very much) the pitch of sound produced.

Although the common image of a percussion-playing child may be of a robust jolly boy bashing away at a big drum with a daft grin all over his face, playing percussion properly has little to do with banging drums and tinkling chime bars.

Learning classical percussion is best suited to tense, obsessive children with a lot of nervous energy. Here, their natural tension is both harnessed and sublimated in the business of counting bars of rest for minutes at a time and then delivering one delicate and precise tap on the side drum or a single stroke on a gong – of precisely the right intensity and at the right millisecond.

Many excellent professional percussionists do not have a good sense of rhythm: what they do have is an instinctive delicacy and sense of timing.

Percussion players always aim at mastering a range of instruments. Because to buy all these would become rather expensive, most players are dependent on using the school's, band's or orchestra's larger instruments.

Untuned percussion instruments make a very good second study for pianists who want the chance of getting together with others – any orchestra or band will make room for one more percussionist.

The side drum

The side drum is the key instrument. It can be used in marching bands or treated as an orchestral instrument, with ten or fifteen years (or more!) spent perfecting a side-drum roll. Because it is a very simple machine, it places great demands on the player.

It can surprise parents and teachers how a child who expresses no interest in music will practise the side drum religiously every day in order to rehearse for the weekly band practice and the Sunday morning parade. Like the bugle player, the drummer has a direction in which to go, a career-interest in the instrument.

Nor are Junior Musicians in the Forces restricted to these traditional – or even military band – instruments. In any symphony orchestra, you will find members of every section who began their professional training as Junior Musicians.

Bass drum, tom-toms, bongoes, etc.

The other drums – bass drum, tom-toms, bongoes, etc. – follow on a study of the side drum, but each has its own techniques, its own kind of music.

Restless children who can't stay long in one subject or area of work will find this range of instruments a boon.

Triangle, cymbals and tambourines

The triangle, cymbals and tambourines are the other basic untuned percussion instruments. Much abused by children, each *can* produce a surprisingly extensive range of effects. Mastering the several techniques to be able to reproduce the vast range of effects as required by written music takes endless hours of hard work. Because the individual instruments are small, they can be worked on at home, without disturbing the rest of the family.

Gongs, wood-blocks, maracas, shakers

Gongs, wood-blocks, maracas, shakers and all the other weird bits and pieces which appear from time to time on the percussion stand are surprisingly rewarding. Any one, in the hands of a layman, may give only one unpleasant sound; learning to make several different musical effects is quite satisfying without demanding long-term application.

The drumkit

The drumkit is a complex of instruments, consisting in its basic form of side or snare drum, two tom-toms, a foot-operated bass drum and cymbals both operated by foot and hit with the sticks.

Because of classical prejudice, learning the drumkit is often under-rated. Kits are rarely found in symphony orchestras, except for performances of music by modern composers.

No child should begin by trying to learn the kit as a whole, until he has first become familiar with and reasonably good at the individual instruments, particularly the side drum. Many pop-orientated children take up the drumkit with no previous musical experience or training. The miracle is that for some, the motivation is strong enough to drive them on through all the problems to achieve a good technique, but most fail early and give up, discouraged and thinking they are "no good at music".

Even the kit-players who do make a go of it, often do it all by ear and don't learn to read music, which is a pity, since it means that they are restricted to playing only improvised pop and rock music.

It is possible to buy a student kit for little more than the price of a clarinet, so that the child need not be dependent on borrowed school equipment.

Taking the kit seriously does mean hours of daily practice, on each instrument separately and on the kit itself. Like all the untuned percussion, it requires a reasonably agile body and good wrists. Never play squash against a percussionist!

TUNED PERCUSSION
Xylophone, vibraphone, marimba, glockenspiel

All these instruments are based on the physical layout of the piano keyboard, but they are not mechanised, so that the player himself has to hit the metal or wooden bars to produce the sound. To play chords with several sticks in each hand is exceptionally difficult and requires hours of absorbing practice on each piece of music. The problem is that this usually has to be done at school, where the instrument is, rather than when the child feels like practising, at home.

The glockenspiel and xylophone are used in orchestral music; the marimba is most at home in Latin-American music and the "vibes" (a kind of electrified xylophone) produces the cool vibrato associated with Modern Jazz.

A child who has not already learnt some piano technique will find these instruments doubly hard, but they are excellent, though rarely-thought-of, second studies for pianists.

The timpani

The timpani (or kettledrums) are a pair or set of drums which are tunable to different pitches by the player. They are extremely difficult to play well but have a worse reputation than they merit, due to the fact that many of those who take them up have had their grounding in untuned percussion where they have never had to train the ear.

The problem of tuning these instruments, keeping them in tune and changing the tuning to match the orchestra is a real strain. Not for nothing, the usual posture of the timpanist when not playing is crouched over one of the drums, anxiously tuning and re-tuning.

The timpanist must be conscientious, obsessive and *very* musical. If intending to play much, the young timpanist will need parents with a van to transport the gear.

The timpanist is cut off from the rest of the orchestra, physically by the effective barrier of the timps which hedge the player round, and mentally because nobody in any section of the orchestra will understand the special problems. Occasionally found elsewhere, the timpanist's true home is on the throne-like rostrum presiding over a full symphony orchestra.

Orchestral chromatic timps are prohibitively expensive to buy, so most schools and youth orchestras make do with two or three simple timps each tuned to play one note – but they still have to be kept in tune!

The positive way – keyboard instruments

The piano

This instrument is still suffering from a hangover. Because Victorian households required a piano as a status symbol – much like today's colour television – and as a core for the amateur music-making which was then common, far too many children of my and previous generations were "put to the piano", because, like Everest, it was there. The failure rate was, understandably, disastrous.

For the right child, learning the piano is still the best single grounding in the theory and practice of music. Its one big **defect** – remediable by the teacher – is that playing the piano does nothing to develop one's ear.

But which is the right child? The piano demands a quick, mental-arithmetic-type brain and a good memory. (The child who can't memorise a phrase or group of notes is not best suited to the piano and should be directed to a single-note instrument, like the flute or clarinet). A pianist must be naturally studious and prepared to practise. (On the piano, there's no cheating: you have either learned a piece or you haven't.)

A social, outgoing child will be miserable on the piano, because there are few opportunities – certainly in the early stages – to play with others. But this is a marvellous instrument for the self-contained child who is used to being, and playing, alone. The repertoire of music to play – at all stages of learning – is extensive, from simple tunes to classical music, to arrangements, to light and pop music. There is always another book of pleasant arrangements to tackle. Indeed, as with the violin and the guitar, there is a lifetime of classical repertoire playable by the pianist who reaches a reasonable standard.

Apart from the electric instruments, the piano is the most highly-developed musical machine. The machine itself pitches the notes, so there is never the awful discouragement which awaits the young oboist or violinist – of hearing their early efforts materialise as anti-music! Thus, no musical "ear" is required of the player. Instead, he needs a high degree of mental and physical co-ordination, in order to hit the right keys, as many as ten at a time!

The piano is an excellent therapeutic instrument for children who have suffered a long-term illness. Unlike the wind instruments, it causes no physical stress. The player remains comfortably seated to play. It requires endless hours of quiet concentration and self-discipline.

Without making wild claims for keyboards, many children with respiratory disorders find the piano a consoling hobby during those lonely depressing days which have to be spent indoors. A bedridden child can profit from an electric piano keyboard across the bed, connected to earphones, so as not to disturb the child in the next bed!

Children can start to learn the piano as soon as they can read, have learnt to relate to a teacher, and know that work is different from play.

Any child who wants to write music will find this immeasurably easier if he learns the piano first. Conversely, a child who has made good progress on another instrument and wants to extend his knowledge of music is well advised to take up the piano as a second study – as early as possible.

As a last word of advice, remember that playing piano music is not easy. A child who gives up the piano after a reasonable period of study should be encouraged to try a single-note instrument and will almost always get a tremendous morale-boost when he finds out (a) how much easier it is to play flute, clarinet or whatever, and (b) that all the hard work on the piano has given him a flying start on the new instrument.

The electric keyboard instruments

The electric keyboard instruments – organs, electric pianos and synthesisers – are far too rarely thought of as instruments for children. Since the introduction of solid-state electronics, there is probably less to go wrong with electric instruments than with conventional woodwind instruments. Electric instruments are the victims of classical prejudice. Few musicians or teachers would contemplate a

Using an electric keyboard during a rock workshop

child taking up one of them, because they are usually connected with pop or light music. Precisely because of this connection, many children who couldn't tell a Baroque trio from a symphony orchestra (and there are millions of them) leap at the chance of learning an electric instrument.

They can appear expensive to buy because they require not only the keyboard element but also an amplifier. However, a multi-channel amp can handle several keyboards or combinations of guitars and keyboard, if necessary. Because they are portable, they can be taken around for a child to go out and play with friends – which can't be done with the conventional piano. For the same reason, they have a place in modern homes where the rooms are too small to accommodate a conventional piano, and in flats, where they can be used for practice with headphones which both exclude ambient sound from the player and prevent the neighbours from being disturbed.

They are fascinating for children who are bored with the piano's old-fashioned image or who wish to experiment with sound and not be restricted by the mechanics of the piano. The electric instruments have many different tone and effects controls, allowing the player to make the sound of a clavichord, harpsichord, or piano, to use vibrato and wah-wah and fuzz, etc. Some of them can sound like a complete string section, an accordion, or percussion; others have concrete music and abstract effects switchable at will. They can give a keyboard-trained child endless hours of pleasure, but are not instruments to be tackled lightly by those who have lacked previous training on the piano.

Teenagers who are fascinated by electronics will find it a great joy to take them to bits, and modify and extend the range of possible effects.

Reed- and pipe-organs

These instruments are a bit out of fashion. There's more to organs than the monstrosity hulking in the shadows of the church! It's easy in most parts of the country to find old harmoniums in junk shops at very reasonable prices. They are usually in bad repair but quite workable-on by the average teenager who understands a bit about woodwork.

Keyboard-orientated children are often fascinated by these old instruments. A child with basic training on the piano – particularly one who enjoys singing and taking part in church activities – will get a real thrill out of learning the harmonium and then coming to play the pipe-organ to accompany the choir in church.

Pipe-organs, with their multiple manuals, foot pedals and banks of stops, require human computers to play them, and thus make an absorbing challenge for the studious and well co-ordinated child.

Early keyboard instruments

Harpsichords, spinets and other early keyboard instruments are often a great joy to children who have a feel for early music. Some previous keyboard technique is helpful. A good ear is also necessary for these early designs do not stay in tune. Many amateur harpsichordists spend more time tuning than playing!

Although craftsman-made instruments in these categories are very expensive, there are a number of excellent kits on the market, with carefully chosen wood, excellent quality materials and easy-to-follow directions. A surprising number of older teenagers get good results building these kits, followed by high motivation to play them. Building a kit at school is a good way of involving a number of practical children in a project of musical value and intrinsic satisfaction.

Most of these instruments produce such a small volume of sound as to be almost inaudible by today's levels of listening. We are all accustomed nowadays to too much ambient noise! It's easy, however, to amplify early keyboard instruments by means of a Barcus Berry pickup on the sound-board. The result is not only as much volume as wanted, but also some very original effects.

The positive way – classical guitar

The classical guitar (also called the Spanish guitar and the acoustic guitar) is today's most popular instrument – due to its glamorous image in folk music, its use for self-accompaniment by popular singers, and because it is a first cousin of the electric guitar of the pop and rock worlds.

Because of this, the guitar is devoid of the connotations which put many children off learning violins or other "cissy" instruments and motivation to work hard at learning can be very high, especially in children from non-musical backgrounds and where little parental support is available.

"I always wanted to be a violinist. Passionately. I listened to violin records and even went to concerts. Nobody else from our area ever went to a concert. But I knew that if I'd been seen carrying a violin case about, or if people knew I was having piano lessons, it would get . . . so I couldn't show my face in the street.

"Learning the guitar was okay. You know, the Beatles and all that . . ." (John, aged 18: Grade 8 guitar)

There are two ways of looking at the guitar. Many happy-go-lucky children want to try the guitar because they have seen singers plonking out a few chords on television and it looks easy. Provided they stick to learning a few chords and using a capo, they can enjoy themselves as the life and soul of the party.

Many folk guitarists learn to play by ear and do not bother to learn to read music. So long as the child is certain that all he wants to do is play chords for a sing-song, that's fine. However, children should not be allowed the delusion that you can start to play by ear and then just pick up reading music. Reading guitar parts is *extremely* hard. What tends to happen is that the player-by-ear cannot face "going back to square one" by learning to read and thus remains in a musical impasse, unless he has an exceptional talent for improvisation.

Learning to play classical guitar requires a conscientious, quiet, serious and hard-working temperament, more like that of the pianist or violinist.

It also needs very good physical and mental co-ordination; whereas the piano produces the right note mechanically providing you depress the correct key, to make a note on the guitar requires the left hand to execute difficult and precise patterns, while the right hand plucks the correct string at the right time in the correct manner – and while the eyes are reading music far more difficult than any flute or clarinet or trumpet part.

Chess players seem to make good guitarists.

Any child who bites his nails and gets interested in playing the guitar has to choose one pastime or the other. Chewed-down nails can't play guitars.

The guitar is not an instrument for sociable children (except in folk music). Not only will they be miserable at the long hours of solitary practice which must be put in, but also they will never find much chance of playing together with others – there's very little repertoire.

Much of the work of learning has to be done by the child on his own. This develops his self-discipline which, in turn, often improves school-work generally.

74

11-year-old boy starting on guitar

Particularly during puberty, girls can find the correct guitar posture uncomfortable against the left breast. There is some scanty evidence to connect guitar-playing with mastitis in adolescent girls.

There are many very cheap small-size guitars on the market which encourages schools to buy them – almost by weight! Particularly when thinking about buying a cheap guitar, it's always worth asking the advice of a competent guitarist, preferably the teacher, because some of the cheaper models are wrongly designed and of dimensions which make it impossible ever to tune them properly.

There are three-quarter and half-size guitars available for children who are too small to cope with the full-size instrument. Although some guitarists do start their children earlier, the normal age to begin this physically and mentally demanding instrument is about eight, when the left hand is able to span the first "stretches" and individual fingers are strong enough to hold down the strings on the frets.

Parents who find that a child is doing reasonably well in class guitar lessons are well-advised to try and buy individual lessons. Nobody (so far as I know) would seriously suggest learning the piano in class and the guitar is more difficult to learn, not easier.

Misled by its current glamorous image, many children take up the guitar for the wrong reasons and in the mistaken belief that it is easy. Their disillusionment comes soon, but, as with the piano, the drop-outs should not be allowed to think that this failure means they are no good at music; often, when directed to the simpler single-note instruments, they make rapid progress, capitalising upon all the hard work previously put in on the guitar.

The positive way – electric guitar

The electric guitar is a new instrument, invented just before the Second World War. It is probably more hated by adults and certainly more maligned than any other instrument because of its abuse (or should we call it exploitation?) in the pop world. To study the electric guitar properly and comprehensively takes as much work as studying the classical guitar. Indeed, the best way to achieve a good technique on the electric guitar is first to pursue a course of classical guitar study. Far too many electric guitar addicts model themselves on pop heroes, adopt wrong playing positions, accept appalling finger technique and never find out very much about their wonderful instrument.

After approximately Grade 2 on the classical guitar, a child will be able to find the immense and exciting freedom of *improvising* on the electric guitar, which was designed for the purpose.

It is often overlooked that the use of a practice amplifier producing 5 or 8 or 10 watts of output can make practising the electric guitar acceptable even in most modern homes. Certainly, using an electric guitar in a school practice studio need not produce any more noise than a trumpet or piano.

Very few children have to be led to the electric guitar. Guidance in this respect is probably best kept negative by emphasizing the considerable amount of work that has to go into learning to read music rather than just playing around with electrical tricks like fuzz box, wah-wah pedal and phasers. Fifteen years ago even professional electric guitar players would get away with having only a rudimentary technique, but in the last few years the standards of inventiveness and instrumental competence have risen very, very rapidly. The pity is that it is still extremely difficult for a child to find any formal teacher of technique on this instrument.

Electric
guitar

"I work just as hard on the electric guitar as I do on the classical . . .
people don't understand that the electric guitar is a completely
different instrument, with different techniques, but there are no
examinations for it." (Rick, aged 15 : Grade 5 on classical guitar)

Despite the high initial motivation to learn, lack of good tuition in the
early stages discourages many children and most school music
teachers are hostile to the instrument. (Perhaps because its young
players and fans have not equipped themselves to take up any in-
school role?)

There is no doubt that an electric guitar pupil who is also studying classical guitar and has therefore learned to read music to some extent can easily be integrated in the school band, at the same time providing a focus and a hero figure for the rougher pupils who might otherwise scoff at all instrumental studies.

It is easy for the electric guitarist to convince himself that he doesn't need to learn to read music. Nothing could be further from the truth and nothing more limiting in his eventual exploitation of the instrument. It is a disservice to a child beginning the electric guitar for anybody to encourage this attitude of mind.

There is a slight possibility of suffering injury or death by electric shock, but a device called the "Play-Safe" can be used between the guitar and the amplifier to avoid this risk. In any case, the weight and dimensions of the electric guitar put it out of question for most children younger than eleven or twelve.

The body of the electric guitar is much thinner than that of the classical guitar, so that it is physically more suited to girls' physique than is the classical guitar.

There is so much inspiration to play the electric guitar, but the initial weeks of learning the instrument can be discouraging. Dreams are shattered by sore fingers and aching muscles! I would recommend very strongly that children who want to play this instrument should save up to buy the instrument, even if parents help to buy the amplifier.

Many children who would otherwise be easily discouraged will persevere on an instrument which represents so much hoarded pocket money.

Although the first weeks of learning may be grim, there is an early reward ahead, for, once a few chords have been mastered, the aspiring rock star will find that he can already get together with friends and make a primitive group to play simpler pop music.

Schools which have to buy new instruments should bear in mind that a new electric guitar and an amp powerful enough to play with the school orchestra will not cost more than one good flute.

The positive way – electric bass

The electric bass, or bass guitar, is an even newer instrument than the electric guitar. Because of this, it is even harder – if not impossible – to find tuition. School music teachers may not be able to help much as far as instrumental technique goes, but they can help with the problems of reading bass clef. (Very few students of the electric bass learn to read music because their parts are written in bass clef and for some unaccountable reason people think it is harder to read bass clef than treble clef!)

The four-stringed electric bass, within its normal continuo role (like the tuba or double-bass) does require less brain-work than the six-stringed electric guitar or the classical guitar but has the same high motivation because of the glamour of the pop world. It particularly suits youths who want to play together with others.

An easy-going or pop-conscious, gregarious child is ideally suited to this instrument. Again, as with the electric guitar, it's worth bearing in mind that every amplifier does have a volume-control knob and it's not necessary to shatter the house or intrude on other users of school premises when playing this instrument.

Lesson One at the Bentovim Day School Rock Workshops is always that dynamics are just as important in rock as in classical music. In other words, if you start by playing flat out, you have nowhere left to go!

The electric bass is a low register guitar, not an electric version of the double-bass. Children looking for a second instrument will find it possible to progress very fast on the bass, within the limits of the instrument.

In common with the electric guitar, the bass guitar lacks a system of examinations or grades. Therefore there is no certain way in which the student can assess his own progress. Hopefully, this will change in the next few years as bass guitar-players extend the range and capabilities of their instrument and as composers become more aware of the musical possibilities, particularly harmonic possibilities, of this extraordinary instrument.

Heavier than the electric guitar, the bass is not recommended for anyone under thirteen.

The positive way – harp

The orchestral harp is cumbersome, expensive and extremely difficult to learn. Harp technique is like playing a dozen pre-set guitars with two right hands!

The harp child will be quite certain about wanting to play this instrument, without any question of doubt or need for encouragement.

The Celtic (Welsh or Irish) harp is far more likely to appeal to children. There are no foot-pedals to operate, the range is smaller, and the music which is available is part of the folk world, with its own particular charm. Even Celtic harps which have to be custom-made are expensive. Orchestral harps cost thousands of pounds.

Other instruments

The instruments listed above cover most of the range in which children are likely to show an interest for leisure use. There are also many other instruments which particularly recommend themselves for individual children, for a combination of family, social or cultural reasons.

These include the ethnic instruments, such as bagpipes, squeeze-boxes, penny-whistles, sitars, steel drums. There may be problems in finding a teacher, but these are more likely to be solved by the local Community Relations Officer than by the musical establishment.

Children on these instruments can find it frustrating not to have any exams to work for, but this may be offset by the impetus of following in a family, or cultural, musical tradition.

The fretted instruments, such as banjoes, mandolins, ukeleles (but not guitars) have their own musical society (small "s"), like that of the brass bands. There are regular meetings of fretted-instrument clubs, frequent get-togethers, and competitions and annual festivals in which children can enter for many different classes. Competitive, gregarious children derive a lot of enjoyment from playing these instruments and taking part in these events. It is usually difficult to find a good teacher.

Singing

Today, singing no longer means a choice between light opera and folk music. Most of the heroes of the pop world are singers – of one kind or another.

However, training the voice and receiving classical tuition in vocal technique does not really come into this book. The world of the chorister is a specialised field. Otherwise, vocal training does not begin before late adolescence. For the majority of children, singing means working on folk songs and the new pop cantatas – a happy way of passing school music lessons.

"When can I begin"

Opinions differ as to the ages when children can begin the different instruments. As always, we have to depend upon the instinctive discretion of the parent or teacher concerned, bearing in mind the physical and mental development of the child.

I would always err on the late side, because of the stress which many instruments can place on a child's growing body, but, against that, the decision to learn has to follow closely upon the initial inspiration.

Children who begin a little young on instruments will always need a lot of parental support. This is not the same as "pushing" the child. It is far better to let a young child make seemingly very slow progress and enjoy himself than to force the pace and take away some of the pleasure of learning.

Below is a rough table of the ages at which I recommend children can start the instruments mentioned in this Section.

There is no harm at all in letting young children who are interested, explore what it feels like to blow, scrape and hit musical instruments. It's quite fun to make up your own simple tunes on the recorder, even if nobody else considers them of any musical merit! But for most children, the *business* of learning an instrument shouldn't begin before the sixth birthday. It's difficult to generalise because many six-year-olds are taller than some nine-year-olds, but for a child of average physique, the following instruments are available:

At 6	Sopranino recorder (for small hands), descant recorder (for larger hands), untuned percussion (drums, triangles, tambourines, etc.), tuned percussion (xylophones, chime bars), quarter-size violin, piano.
At 7	Half-size 'cello, half-size classical guitar, button accordion.
At 8	Tenor recorder, half-size violin, cornet.
At 9	Piccolo, folk guitar (playing chords), tenor horn, other squeeze-boxes, folk instruments generally.
At 10	Flute, clarinet, trumpet, baritone horn (and other brass-band instruments, depending on the size of the child).
At 11/12	Oboe, bassoon, alto sax, harp, viola, drumkit, timpani, electric piano, electric guitar.
13 onwards	Double-bass, bass guitar, trombone, French horn, tuba, synthesiser, harpsichord (and other early keyboard instruments).

Section 6
Getting Started: Advice on Finding an Instrument

Once a child has been inspired, has made the conscious decision to learn, and has been helped to choose the instrument which corresponds with his physical, mental and emotional characteristics, the next stage is to find a teacher and an instrument on which to learn.

There are four ways of finding the instrument:

> buying a new one;
> buying second-hand;
> hire-buy;
> borrowing.

Buying a new instrument

It is always a good idea to have the teacher's, or a musician's, advice when buying the instrument. However, many children are so excited at the prospect of possessing their own instrument (a real one, not a toy) that they – and the parents – can't wait to go and buy it.

This is understandable, for the act of purchasing is not simply a material acquisition; it is a symbol of the child's decision to learn and the parents' involvement in, and support of, this decision.

Perhaps the cost of the instrument seems high to non-musicians, but it's worth bearing in mind that money spent in purchasing an instrument is never lost. There will always be other people who want to buy a second-hand instrument and even if the child eventually gives up and loses interest (and leaving aside the benefits he may have gained while he was learning), the instrument can usually be sold without any great trouble to a music shop, or privately, for at least a sensible proportion of the initial outlay. Unless damaged, the rate of depreciation is far slower than for bicycles or cars.

In some cases – but this tends to happen only with the more expensive instruments which are of a better than average quality – the instruments may even have appreciated in value in the meantime. Instruments only *seem* to cost a lot when viewed in isolation. I often ask children at concerts whether they think that £90 is a lot of money to spend on a flute and almost without exception they chorus: "Yes!". Then I ask how many of them have bicycles which cost £75 or more. About fifty per cent of the hands go up, even in areas which are far from prosperous. It all boils down to a value judgement; whether the parents or other purchasing adults consider that a musical instrument is worth as much as a bicycle or a holiday abroad.

There is so much mystique surrounding the whole business of music that non-musicians going to buy an instrument often fail to ask questions which they would automatically ask when buying a refrigerator or a new car. Yet those who deal in instruments find nothing strange about being asked for trade-in prices or what servicing and repair facilities are available and whether one brand or another is better value for money.

Perhaps none of us likes to appear ignorant and the non-musician feels that in a music shop every question he asks betrays his ignorance. It's better to put false pride completely aside and ask as many questions as you like. You will offend no one and may do yourself and the child a big favour.

If you can't find a musician or music teacher to ask for advice, then the best rule of thumb is to go to one of the larger music shops which is more liable to have a choice of instruments. Quite often *the child* will be able to tell by comparing the feel of the instruments, or by the sound which they produce, which is the better buy – even if he has never tried one before.

Purchase on approval

If the parent is unsure, the shop will normally agree to the child's trying the instrument for a short period, before making the sale "final". This buying on approval is a recognised system of buying musical instruments. From an unknown client, the shop may insist on a cheque which will not be cashed for a week. A period of a few days is usually sufficient for the parent or the child to take the instrument to the teacher, literally for "approval". He or she will be able to point out any obvious mechanical defects or problems like pads which do not quite cover holes, unevenness of frets, varnished-over cracks in woodwork and so on.

Hire-purchase

Most music shops will be happy to supply instruments on a hire-purchase agreement of one kind or another and be equally prepared *at the time of purchase* to discuss what "trade-in" price they will allow in the event that the instrument is not continued with beyond a set period.

Short-term hire-purchase for periods of less than a year does not normally carry any interest payments.

Hire-and-buy

The best way of buying a new instrument for a child (or an adult) is the hire-and-buy system operated by most reputable music shops.

It works this way: you hire a new instrument for a period of three months or longer at a set cost per month. The monthly rate is between five per cent and ten per cent of the total purchase price. If the child decides after the initial period that he is not interested in playing that particular instrument, you can return it to the shop with no further obligation after paying the agreed hire price. On the other hand, if you wish to buy the instrument, the shop will deduct the hire fee paid from the purchase price.

For many reasons, most of them obvious, it is very unusual to hire an instrument for longer than this sort of trial period. Hire charges soon mount up to the cost of buying the instrument and the problems for a shop in running any kind of comprehensive hiring service would make the idea uneconomic.

Whilst an instrument is in your home under a "hire-and-buy" agreement, it is important to establish whose is the duty to insure it, since it may not be covered by your own household contents insurance. All sorts of accidental damage, apart from theft or total loss, can easily happen. I've had many anguished telephone calls from parents of children who have sat on their flutes and bent them into extraordinary and unplayable shapes – and parents whose children have chipped, however slightly, the varnish on a hired guitar or violin. Bear in mind that children have to learn how to assemble their instruments and how to look after them and it is comparatively simple in the early stages to bend a rod or even split the barrel of a woodwind instrument. Central heating and the resultant dryness in the atmosphere inside many family homes can cause warping and splitting of woods.

Buying second-hand

Buying second-hand instruments – like buying second-hand cars – can reduce outlay considerably, but guidance from a professional person is essential, in the same way as one would normally get the R.A.C. or the A.A. to vet a second-hand car.

If, for whatever reason, no professional advice is available, it remains the obvious and safest course to go to a reputable music shop with a servicing department and get a *new* instrument which will be guaranteed by the maker or the shop for a reasonable period.

There are, generally speaking, three markets (each with its own price level) for buying and selling second-hand instruments: music shops, private individuals and junk shops.

Obviously, the safest place to buy second-hand is in a music shop. It's worth listening to the owner if he tries to steer you away from his selection of second-hand instruments towards the new ones, because he knows that children are not rational about this business of getting their own instrument. A lot of children feel cheated if they get an instrument which has *obviously* been used before.

There are few owners of music shops whom I have ever encountered who are in the game solely for money. Someone who knows enough about music and instruments to run a shop successfully will almost certainly be a music-lover who wants to do everything possible to get children off to a good start.

Buying a second-hand instrument from a private individual, usually a child or an adult who has given up using it, should be cheaper than buying from a shop. Most people will tell you the true history of the instrument, how much use it has had, any defects it may have and so on. Newspaper advertisements and that extraordinary magazine *Exchange and Mart* can be useful so long as you can get a professional opinion on the goods which are offered for sale.

Junk shops are not bad for string instruments, guitars or brass instruments but are usually disastrous for woodwind. *Caveat emptor!* As a very rough rule of thumb, one can say that the greater the number of moving parts in an instrument, the greater the risk attached to buying a second-hand one: since there are no moving parts in a violin, there is no hidden hazard in buying a second-hand violin, but clarinets and other woodwind instruments have so many moving parts, springs, rods, tensed screws and pads that there are many, many more things to go wrong.

The piano is probably the only instrument where there is a colossal and overriding financial argument in favour of buying second-hand. New pianos cost hundreds and even thousands of pounds, but it is still possible to buy a perfectly satisfactory second-hand piano, and move it and tune it, all for less than £100. This is largely because so many older people who've had a piano for years, but no longer play it, want the space in their home or move into a smaller house upon retirement and can't afford to accommodate the piano any longer. It's very worth while finding a tuner whom you will eventually employ to tune the piano in your house and asking him to make a paid examination before you buy second-hand.

Long-term borrowing

If it is impossible for a child to have his own instrument, there are several methods of borrowing long-term:

> through the school;
> through a junior orchestra or band;
> from a brass band;
> from an educational music centre.

A lot of instruments borrowed through schools have appalling defects, due to neglect and mishandling by previous borrowers. As with buying second-hand, the more moving parts in an instrument, the greater the likelihood of damage. Unfortunately, many school music teachers and peripatetic teachers know little about the mechanics of instruments and nobody can be expert in all instruments.

Thus, I meet many children at Bentovim Day Schools playing on borrowed instruments which break my heart. All too often, the child has come to think he has a grave fault in technique, when it is the instrument which is damaged. Because they are not involved in what the child is doing in the way in which a parent who has helped to buy an instrument *must* be involved, few parents think of paying the local music shop to repair a borrowed instrument. And yet, the cost of replacing a few pads or putting in a new spring will only be a couple of pounds.

Another problem of borrowing through the school is that, when the child leaves the school, the instrument is withdrawn, possibly curtailing the child's practical interest in music.

In the North, brass bands have a tradition of purchasing instruments from band funds and lending these to the players, both junior and adult. Elsewhere, junior orchestras and Saturday-morning Music Centres run by the Education Department have a small stock of instruments available for long-term loan.

It does seem that a child playing on a borrowed instrument is at some disadvantage, inasmuch as he has not had the chance of "materialising" his decision to learn, nor have his parents demonstrated their support of that decision and their involvement in what he is doing by spending money to give him his own instrument. Teachers and parents often fail to take into account that a child *wants* to save up to buy – or at least contribute towards the cost of – a coveted instrument.

The best use of borrowed instruments is to enable many children, who wouldn't otherwise get the chance, to have an extended trial of the instrument they think they want to play. Whenever possible, as soon as a child has demonstrated an aptitude to play and willingness to work (implying the decision to learn), he should have his *own* instrument.

Getting Started: Advice on Finding a Teacher

There are four places where children can have lessons:

> at school
> at an Education Department Music Centre
> at a private Music School
> with a private teacher

The school system

In some areas of Britain, instrumental tuition is available for children in Primary Schools, but in most places it is restricted to children who have already transferred to Middle or Secondary Schools.

Instrumental tuition is not normally the business of the in-school music teacher. He does general class music and prepares his children in theory and harmony studies for GCE and CSE examinations. He also has an advisory function and should be able to "tap" the system for instruments and lessons.

Instrumental tuition is normally given in State schools by peripatetic teachers, deployed by the local Music Adviser to travel among the schools in his area. Each peripatetic tends to teach not one instrument but a group of "allied" instruments. Except in the field of woodwind, where, as we have seen, there are significant differences between the various instruments, this is a system which can work reasonably well. Woodwind children are often unhappy when taught by a peripatetic whose first instrument is not their own. Understandably, players of reed instruments are often ignorant of flute technique and the problems of flute-playing . . . and vice versa.

Depending upon the number of peripatetics available and the number of children wanting to learn particular instruments, a child may find himself having exclusive attention in a one-to-one situation – or he may be one of up to eight children sharing a lesson.

These lessons are provided free as a part of the State education programme. They do not continue during school holidays.

It is often a matter of chance and/or tradition whether these lessons are available at a given school. Therefore, if the Head Teacher or music teacher says that tuition is not available on the instrument which a child has chosen to learn, it is *always* worth a parent arguing the child's case to have a peripatetic come to the school just for that child. (Perhaps there are other children wanting lessons, whose parents are too passive to argue.) The parents can always write to, or telephone, the Music Adviser if the school is not helpful. The motto should always be to argue in defence of the child's choice, rather than suit the convenience of the system and push the child on to an instrument in which he is not really interested.

Many children feel that music is a very private part of their lives and lose interest when taught in a class situation. This may be inconvenient of them, but it happens.

"It's difficult to explain, but music is very private. At least, it is for me. In a class at school, it's like having to do it in public. I'd like to have lessons on my own." (Michelle, aged 12 : Grade 3 flute)

A compromise is for the child to have some individual lessons, interspersed with class lessons.

On the positive side, a lot of children from non-musical backgrounds feel quite at ease having music lessons at the school, whereas they might feel embarrassed to admit to their friends that they were going to a private teacher for lessons. Also, competitive children can really enjoy the presence of the other children.

"Playing with other people is great. You try to outdo everybody else!" (David, aged 13 : Grade 3 cornet)

The greatest argument in favour of this system is that it spreads the available teaching effort in the widest possible way, enabling many children, who would not otherwise have a chance, to start learning an instrument.

In short, this is a system which can work well for less demanding, out-going children who can make fair progress in the early stages; shy, withdrawn children are unlikely to do well. For a combination of reasons, the drop-out rate from class-learning is very high and few children progress far.

A small number of Education Departments run "studentship" schemes. Children with definite aptitude on a particular instrument (but not necessarily prodigies) are awarded a studentship whereby the Department pays the fees for the child to have lessons from an approved private music teacher. The child is reassessed annually, both to make sure that he is receiving proper tuition and that he is working satisfactorily. This is a system which produces excellent results.

Education Department Music Centres

A recent development within the education system, designed to cope with some of its shortcomings, is the establishment of a small number of Music Centres. Their geographical distribution is haphazard.

Directly or indirectly, they are run by the local Music Adviser, although some of them have a full-time Co-ordinator.

Some Centres have their own premises; others operate in school buildings on Saturday mornings and certain weekday evenings.

The main function of the Centres is to provide, for children learning within the State system, orchestral and choir practice under the guidance of peripatetics. Some include band-work. One or two do jazz. Most children enjoy getting together with friends and children from other schools in this way.

Some Centres also provide instrumental tuition, usually given by peripatetic staff. Even those which do not should be able to advise parents about the local private and State facilities for learning instruments.

Private lessons at school

It is sometimes possible (usually in privately-financed schools) for children to have one-to-one lessons in instrumental technique from a private teacher paid either directly by the parents or by the school, in which case it is added to the bill at the end of term.

Sometimes, these private teachers are not as highly qualified as the State peripatetics, but, because they are giving the child individual attention and because the parents are financially involved, they can be very successful.

Private Music Schools

Many towns have privately-run Music Schools. Because these are unsubsidised, they have usually grown in response to local needs. They would not otherwise survive.

Some are run as schools offering a formal syllabus covering a range of instrumental, theory, choral, orchestral and other activities such as end-of-term concerts. Others are no more than a postal address for the individual private teachers, and premises where they can hire a room in which to give lessons.

Parents seeking private lessons are well advised to begin their quest for a teacher at the local Music School.

Steel band rehearsing at Manchester North Music Centre
Young brass players recording at a Merseyside Music Centre

The private teacher

The traditional way of learning a musical instrument, which is still – to judge by results – more effective than any other, is by buying regular weekly lessons from a private teacher. Where this is beyond the financial means of the family, the parents can very often go to the local Music Adviser and find that the child is eligible for a Studentship grant to cover fees. In order to justify the grant, the Authority will require that the child is already learning and making good progress.

It's worth examining briefly why the system of private tuition continues to produce most of the children who make the best progress in instrumental studies. (Sections 9, 10 and 11 give a much more detailed analysis of the learning process and the changing teacher/pupil relationship). The essential elements of the situation where parents are buying private lessons, are as follows:

1   The child learns in an exclusive one-to-one relationship. He does not have to share the teacher's time or attention with anybody else.

2   The child feels "special" because of this exclusive attention from a respected and often idolised adult. This, in turn, gives a sustained subsidiary motivation to work.

3   The teacher is able to progress each pupil at the rate which suits that child's individual personality and aptitudes.

4   Very few parents will pay for regular weekly lessons and yet take no interest in what is going on. Therefore, the degree of parental involvement and support is usually high.

5   The activity is not just another school "period". The child travels to the lesson mentally preparing for it, and travels away again with the time to digest all that has happened during the time of the lesson.

6   Because this is an activity taking place in free, leisure time, the child is constantly reaffirming the conscious decision to learn by each minor decision to go to a lesson.

7   The teacher is economically motivated. If he isn't good and loses too many pupils, he's going to be hungry.

It's worth remembering that most in-school music teachers, peripatetic teachers of instrumental technique and music advisers have themselves had private lessons in their own childhood and therefore try to incorporate some of the above elements in the facilities available for children learning through the school system. In various towns, for example, the children are sent, sometimes during school hours, to the Music Centres for their instrumental lessons.

Finding a private teacher is rarely easy and may be very difficult.

At present, in Britain, there is no hard-and-fast way of finding a teacher on a particular instrument or of assessing how good any teacher may be for your child.

The only nationwide register of music teachers is operated by the Incorporated Society of Musicians, an organisation of professional musicians, which will be pleased to send a list of its teaching members in your area. The address to write to is:

> The Secretary,
> Incorporated Society of Musicians,
> 10 Stratford Place,
> London, W1N 9AE

Most professional musicians belong to the Musicians' Union and since many of them give private lessons, it is worth contacting the London office of the M.U. to find the name and address of the branch secretary in your area. For the price of a stamped-addressed envelope, he will send a list of the M.U. members who live near you, together with a note of which instruments they play. Write in the first instance to:

> The General Secretary,
> Musicians' Union,
> 29 Catherine Place,
> London, SW1E 6EH

If neither of these national sources provides the answer, the following is a useful check-list to work through, leaving out the suggestions which are obviously inappropriate to your area:

> ask advice from the music teachers of the local schools;
>
> telephone or write to the Music Adviser, who will be based at the local Education Offices;
>
> visit your local Music Centre and ask advice from the Co-ordinator or the Senior Peripatetic Teacher;
>
> contact any peripatetic teacher and ask his advice (many peripatetics give private lessons in their own time);
>
> go to the local School of Music on Saturday morning;
>
> ask the Librarian at the public library, who may well keep a list of music teachers;

visit the local music shops (a good shop knows most of the local teachers, some of whom may give lessons in studios on the shop premises);

don't forget the local press which may have advertisements by local teachers (if it doesn't, place an advertisement yourself, asking for lessons);

check the Music Teachers' section in the Yellow Pages;

never be shy about asking any music teacher to recommend a colleague on the instrument you want;

if there is a child in your neighbourhood making good progress on another instrument, ask for the name and address of his teacher, who may be able to help;

ask the Music Officer of your Regional or sub-Regional Arts Association, who ought to know about many of the performing musicians in the area;

ask any cultural centre, even if not directly concerned with music (e.g. theatre, arts centre) to put you in touch with some professional musicians who may eventually lead you to a teacher;

try going to any nearby professional or amateur orchestra and ask advice from the players (they had to learn somewhere!);

contact the secretary of any local Music College, College of Education, Polytechnic, University or other Further Education College (if the syllabus includes music, there are probably both teachers and students who give private lessons).

Non-musical parents are understandably apprehensive at the thought of buying music lessons from music students or older schoolchildren who have reached Grade 7 or 8 on their instruments. They need not be. Music is unlike any other course of study and it is quite possible for a sixteen-year-old who has been well taught, to be an *excellent* teacher for a young beginner.

(I was teaching the flute before I was fifteen and, by my eighteenth birthday, had teaching practices in three different towns, totalling over forty pupils – many of them older and considerably taller than myself!)

Remember that if a young teacher has a problem with which he can't cope, he'll certainly ask the advice of his own teacher.

Laymen can be confused by the letters – or lack of them – after a teacher's name. The most common qualifications are ARCM,

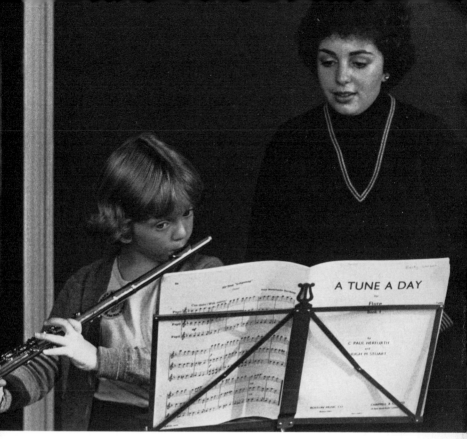

It is quite possible for a 16-year-old to be an excellent teacher
for a young beginner

LRAM, ATCL, LGSM, ALCM. However, many of the best teachers
are graduates or have been to a teacher-training college (with its own
diploma and letters!) or simply never bothered to sit for a diploma.

Word-of-mouth is a good recommendation, always.

Once a teacher has been found, it is *very* difficult for any parent to
know whether the teacher is right for the particular child. Very often,
children get so much from the relationship with a particular teacher
that it is better for them to stay with that teacher rather than to go on
to somebody with more progressive methods or who would
accelerate their rate of progress. The best rule of thumb is that as long
as the child makes progress, is happy with the teacher, practises
regularly without too much argument and looks forward to lessons as
important events, then the teacher is the right one.

Section 8
Musical Snakes and Ladders

Ideally, then, the child

> has been inspired to want to play;
> has made the conscious decision to learn;
> has been matched with the right instrument;
> has found an instrument to learn on;
> has found a teacher.

He is now equipped for the first steps in learning an instrument, which is the most effective way of coming to understand music.

Learning an instrument is unlike any other process of learning: on the one hand it is so technical, and progress is so assessable, almost from day to day; on the other hand, it is so diffuse – involving, requiring and contributing to the developing mental, physical and emotional identity of the child.

To a musically-uneducated parent, it is all a great mystery; to many musicians, it is a process where intuition and tradition stand in place of logic and system; to many teachers, it is an area in which the priorities are unclear.

In discussing such a complicated, diffuse, yet technical, process, I offer the reader a useful analogy. A schematic of the process of learning a musical instrument may be likened to a Snakes and Ladders board. There are three ladders which have to be scaled in the correct order. Stepping from one ladder to the next is not a simple movement, for there are snakes, down which one may slide, not all the way to square one, but to a square called "discouragement".

The first ladder takes the pupil to a position of familiarity with the instrument and basic knowledge of its technique sufficient to be able to play not just a simple tune or a few pieces from the *Tune A Day* book, but a genuine, albeit simple, piece of music. He understands rhythm, has some rudimentary knowledge of musical theory, has started aural training and can read music to the extent of being able to play very simple pieces at sight.

This approximates to the first Grade of the Associated Board's examination scheme – a notional "Grade 1".★

★ For some instruments, the Associated Board's examination grades actually start at Grade 3.

The second ladder lifts the pupil to a new confidence which enables him to play in front of others and play *with* them.

He has mastered the range of the instrument, can read at sight, has a well-rounded knowledge of theory and a reasonably developed ear.

He could take the Associated Board's Grade 5 examination (Instrumental and Theory) and pass the performing part of the GCE 'O' level or CSE examination.

Any child, with the right tuition and guidance, can get to the top of the second ladder. By this time on the game board, all the snakes are behind him. He's done pretty well to get so far and if he doesn't want to go further, he is immeasurably better equipped to enjoy music as a leisure activity than his friends who didn't start the climb.

The third ladder brings the pupil to a position of ability to make true music – not in the sense of becoming a professional performer, but with the instrument so much within his grasp and the theory of music so absorbed that he can take a full part in amateur music-making and think of taking up a career which requires a peripheral knowledge of music.

This is somewhere about the level of the Associated Board's Grade 8 examination or the performance part of GCE 'A' level.

In any game of Snakes and Ladders, there are one or two special ladders which lift one swiftly from the bottom row of squares almost to the end of the board. In our analogy, these are reserved for children of genuine individual talent, the prodigies of this world – with whom this book is not concerned. (There are always musicians, teachers and patrons only too eager to help a prodigy move fast up one of the special ladders.)

For the rest of us, it is possible to miss out one or the other rung, but you do so at your peril! If you don't quite make it to the rung above, you're liable to fall down off the ladder altogether. Indeed, if you're given a faulty ladder which has one or two rungs missing, the likelihood is that you'll fall right through the hole where the missing rungs should be.

Beware! The most difficult ladder is the first.

Section 9
The First Ladder: Getting to Notional Grade 1

> "The first ladder takes the pupil to a position of familiarity with the instrument and basic knowledge of its technique sufficient to be able to play not just a simple tune or a few pieces from the *Tune A Day* book, but a genuine, albeit simple, piece of music. He understands rhythm, has some rudimentary knowledge of musical theory, has started aural training and can read music to the extent of being able to play very simple pieces at sight.

> "This approximates to the first Grade of the Associated Board's examination scheme."

More children fall off the first ladder than off both the other two. This is partly simple arithmetic, because more set out to climb it, but it is also because they are learning the business of ladder climbing, with its essential ingredients:

> a prior conscious decision to learn;
> a constructive teacher/pupil relationship;
> a balanced and comprehensive foundation of learning;
> regular practising;
> parental support.

The teacher/pupil relationship

Such is the nature of a child's natural enthusiasm that many children cannot wait to get started. They have the instrument and they didn't buy it in order to leave it in the case or just to look at it.

Impelled by their initial enthusiasm, they pick it up and begin to find out how it works – perhaps with the aid of a simple primer which gives basic technical points, usually supported by drawings or photographs. These enable the child to go through the motions of playing a number of tunes.

There is no doubt that it is a wonderful and mystifying thing for any non-musical parent to hear his or her child playing the first, recognisable tunes. That is not a disparaging remark; it is a constant wonder to me, too, every time I hear a child begin to make music, however simple.

But parents should beware of allowing their natural instinct (to encourage the child) to distract them from the urgent business of finding a teacher. The child without a good teacher is almost certain to acquire bad habits of technique. An acquired habit is difficult to eradicate. Far better not to acquire it in the first place.

There is very little progress which most children can achieve, beyond the level of playing a few simple tunes, without a strong and constructive teacher/pupil relationship. Finding a teacher is not a job to be put off.

The teacher, for his part, has to bear in mind that a one-to-one learning relationship is a new and exciting experience for the beginner pupil. The initial superficial excitement of possessing an instrument and having one's own teacher will inevitably subside a little. When it does, the relationship has to be such that the pupil will unquestioningly work for the teacher's approval.

It is the habit of working for the teacher's approval which establishes the patterns of discipline which eventually become self-discipline.

To achieve this relationship, the teacher has to assess each pupil both as an individual and in relationship with the instrument. No teacher should, for his own convenience, decide on an arbitrary rate of progress which would enable an ideal child to pass such-and-such an examination after a certain number of lessons, because music is not simply logical or mathematical (although it does use both logic and mathematics).

It is not a contradiction to this, that the teacher must have very firmly in his mind both the essence and the details of the essential learning which has to be absorbed by every child on the first ladder.

Teaching children at this stage, with the extraordinary, rapid progress which they seem to make, can be very exciting, but it is important – particularly for young teachers – not to be carried away by the excitement of teaching "brighter" children, to the extent that they fail to lay down the foundation of essential learning. Every child accepts the necessity for what might seem boring chores, if they are an integrated part of the learning process, implicit in the correct relationship with the teacher.

The teacher has to discover what was the original inspiration for each pupil and keep alive the echoes of that inspiration until, by a subtle process of transference, he becomes the pupil's source of inspiration. This enables him to encourage, control and direct the pupil's natural enthusiasm and to use, so far as possible, the energy and initiatives which are within the child rather than "pushing" the child. There are times when "pushing" is necessary, but not at this stage.

Later, there will be times when the child must be wary of the teacher's influence, but the first ladder will only be scaled in the blind belief that the teacher is right and with the teacher's overt approval for work which has been done, and which has to be done.

Essential learning

So many adults say: "I learnt the piano for three years and now . . . I can't read a note of music."

Why?

Because they never made it up the first ladder: they were not learning the instrument, they were not learning about music; they were being trained to play a few examination pieces, by rote.

Any child can cheat on the learning system with a lazy teacher or in a class situation by memorising tunes, but this is no more than training a dog to do a few party tricks. It is in the end – which will come sooner rather than later – sterile and boring. Time spent on learning to play a few tunes, unrelated to a broader study of music, is pointless.

Whatever the instrument being studied and however easy or difficult its technical demands, the first ladder (or course of study) must cover the following essential areas of learning:

the correct physical relationship with the instrument;
the quality of sound;
aural training;
theory;
reading music and "sight-reading";
understanding rhythm;
how to practise.

These areas of study are not to be tackled sequentially, nor are they in themselves the rungs of the ladder. It is impossible to simplify a subject like music into a number of successive areas of study. It is part of the skill of a teacher of music to lead the pupil from one area into another and back to the first and thence into a third and so on. To begin with, the pupil understands little of the inter-relationship of the various areas of study. But the teacher must be aware that they exist and must give attention to each area all the time, not postponing theory until the pupil is fluent on the instrument or ignoring the quality of sound until the child is playing complicated pieces.

He does this by setting a series of short-term goals. Thus, the pupil is unaware that he is learning theory or grappling with the abstract concept of rhythm, but simply that the teacher wants him to practise these particular exercises and have them perfect by next week's lesson. The world-wide success of the *Tune A Day* series is due entirely to its application of this business of giving children a succession of short-term goals to work for, interleaving rhythm exercises and theory tests and sight-reading and simple duets imperceptibly between the pieces.

If any one area should be tackled first, it is the question of the correct physical relationship with the instrument.

The correct physical relationship with the instrument

There is a correct way of holding and playing each musical instrument. Instruments were not designed ergonomically, to suit the human body. Dimension and design are dictated by the type and range of sound which has to be produced. Some instruments accommodate a natural posture of the human body reasonably well; others require the pupil to acquire a special posture for playing.

Teachers and professional musicians themselves often have very bad posture problems, because they have never learnt how to hold the instrument without causing muscular stress. Changing the posture once you have been playing for a while can be extraordinarily difficult, so it is always better for the teacher to ensure patiently from the first lesson that the child is comfortable on the instrument and holding it in a way which will not inhibit technique.

But, there is more to this than just the way you sit (or stand) and hold the instrument, for you can never develop a good technique on the violin or guitar if you hold the instrument wrongly. Piano technique will not come easily to the child who tries to play with flattened fingers. If you don't learn to breathe properly from the start, you will never make a good quality of sound on a wind instrument.

The quality of sound

The sound is produced directly by the child blowing, scraping, plucking, or hitting some part of the instrument.

Therefore, the *quality* of the sound produced depends upon the way in which the child is operating the instrument. Some children seem completely at home on their instrument and produce a pleasing sound the first time they pick it up; most have to be taught, step by step by the teacher, how to tense or relax particular muscles or sets of muscles, how to adjust the position of the instrument slightly, and so on. Other pupils have to be taught first by the teacher's example how to discriminate between qualities of sound before they know what they are aiming at. The teacher has to instruct the pupil to listen discriminatingly to the sound which he (the pupil) is producing. If the pupil is allowed to continue making a poor quality of sound, he will grow used to hearing this and it will become his normal standard.

That is a hard fault to rectify. When, eventually, he hears other players making a better sound, he will find it extremely difficult, if not impossible, to alter his accustomed physical relationship with the instrument and may well give up playing, due simply to this frustration.

The pupil who has been trained from the beginning to "use his ears" in the process of producing a good quality of sound, is already taking the first steps in the area of aural training.

Aural training

On the Continent, with the traditional emphasis on *solfège*, aural training – training one's ear – is regarded as a prerequisite to any course of instrumental study. In Britain, at the other extreme, the common attitude is to think about giving the child the minimum of aural training two to three weeks before an examination.

This misses the whole point of the exercise. It is not just to pass examinations. Far from it.

There is a certain amount of aural training implicit in most instrumental studies: a brass-player can't pitch his notes without training his ear; a guitarist or string-player can't begin to play until he has tuned his strings by ear.

Unfortunately, a woodwind-player can all too easily assemble the instrument and sit down to play without bothering about tuning. Only later, when he wants to play with others, will he find it excruciatingly difficult to tune to them and stay in tune, because he has not trained his ear.

Few modern children will ever relate to classical music. For them, music is light music, pop and whatever replaces it. If they are deprived of aural training, they will lose any natural ability to "busk" a pop tune with friends, to make up their own improvised music, in short to relate their instrumental studies to their real world of music-for-fun.

In terms of the inter-relationship of the separate areas of learning, aural training is the voice of theory.

Theory

Theory is the grammar of music.

If you live in a foreign country, you can acquire the language by just picking it up, day by day. Prodigies are born natives of the land of music and can "pick it up". For most children, music is a foreign language and they need to acquire the grammar without which the most extensive vocabulary is useless.

If theory is presented as an integral part of every lesson, it is accepted by the child as a natural part of what he is doing. It is only when theory is suddenly presented as an additional, necessary-for-Grade-6, intrinsically rather boring burden, that the child, naturally, resents it. Moreover, the earlier the child starts to do theory, the easier it is (as with learning a foreign language).

Children enjoy games and quizzes and theory is rendered most digestible when presented as a kind of running quiz: a succession of musical questions to be answered without using the instrument.

Many children positively enjoy theory because it relates easily to their non-musical learning experience: arithmetic, reading and the simplicity of a discipline where each question has only one correct answer.

Children who learn a keyboard instrument find theory very easy. They automatically learn to read both clefs and they can see all the notes and chords in front of them as they play.

Children on single-note instruments may find theory more difficult but have a greater need to study and understand in this area because, on these instruments, each note is formed by the player's complicated fingering and it is very tempting to translate the dots on the page directly into a finger position, rather than learning to read music.

Reading music

Because music is non-verbal and non-representational but *has* to be written down by composers and by performers, the system of musical notation has to be, and is, marvellously precise, describing always at least four of the dimensions of music: pitch, rhythm, tempo and dynamics (or loudness).

Because notation is very complicated, the child must learn to read music from the beginning. For the same reason – because it *is* complicated – the beginner is tempted to memorise each piece of music and play it from memory, pretending to glance at the dots. This system of cheating works for the early examinations, but eventually the child will be required to have a repertoire too extensive for memorising, or will be asked to sight-read, or will want to play with others – all with disastrous results!

There are two ways in which the teacher can relieve the pupil of this temptation: the first is to include from the start a small amount of sight-reading in every lesson: in other words, show the child a piece of music he has not seen before and make him attempt to play this on the instrument. The second way is to include in the practice work each week one piece which the child doesn't know and then see what kind of performance of it the child can manage at the next lesson.

In this way, the child comes to see music as sequences of related notes and does not simply translate each written note or chord into a position on the instrument, which is something that can only be done one note at a time. By definition, any child – or adult – playing in *that* way will find it extremely difficult to understand rhythm.

Understanding rhythm

If there is one universal fault, common to poor teachers on any instrument, it is a failure to impart an understanding of rhythm. It is impossible to overstate the gravity of this omission – for a failure to understand (and read) rhythm produces an overall confusion which is the most common cause of children "giving up music".

Ask any ten musicians what rhythm is and you will receive ten different and sometimes conflicting answers. Most of them will be negative, but rhythm is not an abstract concept which stops you doing anything. It is not bar-lines and time-signatures. It is not a precise number of beats to the bar.

All these things have something to do with rhythm, but rhythm is far bigger than all of them.

Rhythm is the way in which music *flows*.

Anything which has to do with the flow of music is rhythmic.

If music did not flow, it would cease to be music.

Isolated, as an abstract concept, an understanding of rhythm is almost impossible for a child to obtain, but taken together with theory, aural training and sight-reading from the outset, it becomes another aid to making music, not an unrelated additional task. A child who cannot understand rhythm cannot read music and play, and is forced to cheat by rote learning and memorising. Written music makes no *sense* to the child who has not learnt the logic of rhythm.

Young pianists do not suffer from this problem as much as those who learn single-note instruments. Their initial progress on the instrument is apparently much slower, so that they spend more time on hundreds of simple tunes, each exemplifying this abstract concept, allowing it to sink gradually into their subconscious. At the other extreme, woodwind players can make rapid progress in instrumental technique which means that they don't go over and over the same simple tunes and therefore tend to hurry on without first grappling with rhythm.

Quite a few children who are not by any means prodigies have an instinctive ability to understand rhythm which enables them to count time with no problems. Usually, these are children with a flair for mental arithmetic. (So far as one can generalise, there are two kinds of intelligence which enable children – or adults – to streak ahead in music: a flair for mathematics and a flair for languages).

But, if you don't understand rhythm, it can seem a thousand times more elusive than pitch.

It is important from the outset that the teacher includes in each lesson some straight rhythm exercises to be played on one note or clapped, so that the child is forced to realise that *notation is as much to convey rhythm as pitch.*

A rhythm exercise should be included in each week's practice schedule.

How to practise

Anybody can tell a child to do half a dozen things before the next lesson, but the beginner pupil needs to be taught how to practise. A good teacher will also subsequently check up from time to time how the child sets about practising, whether it is a regular routine, whether it is interrupted, what rituals the child has invented for himself, etc.

Many teachers make practising more or less like school-taught behaviour, with the pupil keeping a notebook in which is written out the work to be done each week. This should be a balanced diet of pieces to work on, breathing and hand exercises, theory questions, scales, rhythm exercises, etc.

Each individual child should have the right amount of practice activity. Quick workers will get bored and sloppy if they run out of jobs to do and slow ones will be discouraged if too much is put on their plate at once, needing the reassurance of plodding away at the same things until they are perfect.

These notes, plus the teacher's written comments week by week, give the child and his parents a visible record of progress achieved.

What is practising?

Practising is not a meaningless repetition. It is not learning by rote.

Practising is going over and over the same ground many times, in order to transfer new learning from the conscious mind into the subconscious. Only thus do we free the conscious mind for the next input. Failure to practise regularly from the beginning will result in a traffic jam on the conscious level so that unrelated items of information are digested into the subconscious out of context, leading to general confusion. This is a condition very difficult to repair.

At the same time, the physical repetition trains the brain and the body and develops their co-ordination in relation to the instrument. The child must practise to make progress, as anybody can understand. Parents often fail to understand that practice is also necessary even to stand still.

In music, you can't mark time. If you're not moving forward, you're going backwards. This is why many children get discouraged when they have to stop practising during a short illness or holiday. The child assumes that when he begins to practise once again, he'll be able to start where he left off. Instead, he finds unaccountable and very worrying problems: the fingers are stiff and won't do as they're told, the brain doesn't seem to understand the music on the page, pieces which were learnt by heart seem impossible to remember, and so on . . .

It is better for a child to practise ten minutes a day, six days a week, rather than half an hour, once a week. Most beginners will want to spend about ten minutes on their daily practice session and this will build to twenty minutes and maybe half an hour. It is a part of the teacher's function to give each pupil not too little and not too much work to do, to occupy the right amount of practice time each day, for that pupil. If the pupil carries on after practice proper, making up tunes, improvising, or generally playing around with the instrument, that is something else.

Many children invent their own patterns of ritual activity for the regular daily practice session and do twenty hand-stretching exercises, play each scale perfectly ten times, play each piece of music three times without a mistake before going on to the next one. In this way, practice time becomes a kind of personal game with secret rules, a splendid way in which to absorb much of the essential learning.

Parental support

The attitude of the parents to practising has to be a no-nonsense one: that practising is inevitable. They can best help by encouraging the child to make a routine – almost a ritual – of practising, preferably at a regular time each day, e.g. after coming home from school and before sitting down to tea and watching television or doing homework – often, before going to school in the morning. In this way, practice time becomes a normal feature of everyday life. Once a child has got into the habit of practising, he would actually feel there was something wrong with a day when he hadn't practised.

This is not to imply that the happy child never argues about practising. All children play psychological games with their parents, sometimes. But, if a child repeatedly and resolutely refuses to practise, there is something wrong.

Hundreds of times every year, I am accosted by worried parents asking for my help to get their children to practise. Usually, the children have apparently begun well and with great enthusiasm and then suddenly lost interest.

"Should I make him/her practise?" they ask. But this is the wrong question. When I go into the individual case, it's almost always that the child has been influenced to start the piano or the violin because the parents think it would be a nice idea and good for the child. Thus, the child may not have been inspired, has never made the conscious decision to learn, nor has he been matched with the right instrument.

The two questions they should be asking themselves are: "Have we found the right instrument?" and "Have we found the right teacher?"

The child on the right instrument, with the right teacher, is happy to practise, most of the time!

Parents who are close to their children may be disturbed by the intensity of the relationship which quickly develops between the learning child and a good teacher. However, the parent must stand well back. He can boost the child's ego, be an appreciative audience and a constant source of moral support. It is counter-productive and very confusing for the child to have a parent expressing critical judgement. The source of critical judgement must be the teacher. A parent who tries to intervene or give a "second opinion" is undoing a great deal of the teacher's hard work.

There are few incentives which the parent can offer apart from that wonderful medicine: Praise In Large Quantities. Encourage the child to play, however simple the tune, to neighbours, relatives – any audience is better than none. Most children have a natural desire to "show off"! If a beginner wants to take the instrument to school and play to the class or to the local Brownies or Cubs or Guides or whatever, make sure that the instrument is clearly labelled and insured and wish the child good luck – and don't forget to inquire afterwards how the performance went.

No child is too young to learn how to look after his own instrument and transport it safely and with care, and most schools will co-operate by locking the instrument up safely for the rest of the school day.

Parents, too, should take trouble to identify the initial source of inspiration, where this is not already obvious, and sustain it, e.g. by taking the child on visits to concerts by professional and amateur orchestras and chamber groups, or rock concerts, or other entertainment which includes live music.

Parents often overlook the reassurance they can give by simply sitting down to watch a music programme on television with the child and then chatting generally about it, afterwards. Apart from any direct stimulus or information which the child may get from the experience, it is a gesture of parental involvement in what is, for the child, an important sphere of activity and thought.

It's worth enquiring at the local Public Library (not just in the Junior Section) what books there are about musicians and instruments. Few children will actually want to read about "music" at this stage. A child learning an instrument will normally want to build his own private library of records or cassettes which feature the chosen instrument. Even after the first few lessons, the child will understand music better than non-musical parents and consequently get more enjoyment from listening.

Whilst a child is climbing the first ladder, anything the parent can do to place music in its right context as recreation and leisure, is good.

Examinations

Some parents dislike the idea of examinations altogether, believing that their children should not be subjected to this kind of stress.

Some teachers discourage their pupils from sitting examinations, using a variety of arguments, but usually because they resent having to adjust their own schedule of teaching to accommodate the exam syllabus.

My own view is that there is a very small minority of children who should not go in for examinations, because they have abnormally frail personalities. Even these children will probably have to sit examinations in every other field of learning.

Most children actually enjoy the excitement of examinations. The examiner is someone to perform to. The day may be fraught with tension, but not much more so than the day of a geography exam, or a swimming test. Most children suffer from "exam nerves", but learning to cope with this can stand them in good stead, generally.

Any child who is sitting a music examination is usually the centre of family attention for the day – which is always nice.

Most of the recognized musical examination syllabuses are a very useful check system, designed to ensure that the child is following a balanced and comprehensive course of studies.

Providing the child has been properly taught, has covered the necessary ground and worked reasonably hard, he will pass. Because a part of the purpose of these exams is *encouragement*, they allow children who have worked very hard to gain a merit or distinction, which the recipients are justly proud of.

"... it proves you've got somewhere. It makes all the work seem worth while." (Susannah, aged 10: Grade 1 piano)

Conclusion

To render intelligible such a complex process, it is necessary to dismantle it verbally and deal with each aspect separately, but the aspects belong together and the whole is more than the sum of the parts.

A child who reaches the top of the first ladder may still have a long way to go, but nobody who is concerned with his general or musical welfare should deny, or fail to demonstrate appreciation of, the fact that he has already achieved a great deal. The musical establishment, through the examining bodies like the Associated Board, acknowledges this by attesting his success. It is a time for congratulation.

The pupil who gets this far has, however, gained much more than a formal piece of paper. He has done more than simply prepare himself to climb the second ladder. He has acquired some self-discipline, learnt a new language and system of logic, is able to make aesthetic judgements, enjoys an improved co-ordination of body and mind. His general and particular sense of achievement is probaby affecting his school and other work favourably.

Above all, he has always got "something to do", which is greatly more enriching than idly gawping at television.

This is no mean achievement.

Section 10
The Second Ladder: Persevering to Notional Grade 5

> "The second ladder lifts the pupil to a new confidence which enables him to play in front of others and play *with* them.
>
> "He has mastered the full range of the instrument, can read at sight, has a well-rounded knowledge of theory and a reasonably developed ear.
>
> "He could take the Associated Board's Grade 5 examination (Instrumental and Theory) and pass the performing part of the GCE 'O' Level or CSE examination."

There is no plateau or resting place at the top of the first ladder. Children who have climbed it securely, rung by rung, will be in a fluent climbing condition and will step almost imperceptibly from the top rung of the first ladder on to the bottom rung of the second ladder. For them, the second ladder is firm, the rungs are regularly spaced and not too far apart and the gradient is a smooth continuation of what they are used to – even a little easier.

Of course, the Associated Board's Grade 5 standard on guitar or piano or violin is much higher than for wind instruments, but our notional "Grade 5" at the top of our second ladder is a point where the pupil is equipped to enjoy music as a leisure activity and no longer needs to regard it exclusively as a learning process.

Many children step off the first ladder apparently in the direction of the second, only to end up sliding down one of the snakes in between, either because they had cheated in their progress up the first ladder and missed out some significant rungs, or because they were using a badly-constructed ladder.

Other children appear to start well on the second ladder and then, unaccountably, give up. There are two reasons: either the child is on the wrong instrument, so that the satisfactions and rewards for working are irrelevant to that child's needs; or there are gaps in his basic knowledge, which, cumulatively, render it impossible for the child to make any sense out of what he is doing.

Children are not essentially dishonest. After a certain point, those who are badly taught realise for themselves that learning by rote is getting them nowhere along the path to music, although it may have got them through an exam or two. They are right to give up, in their circumstances.

But even they have gained something from the learning process and are better equipped to enjoy music than people who never began to study any instrument. A child who has spent a year or two working on the basics of any instrument has not wasted his time.

Parents who are not themselves educated musically are very much in the dark about what is going on while a child is climbing the second ladder. However obvious it may be to musicians and music teachers that the child is making worthwhile progress from rung to rung, the non-musical parent has to take this on trust, relying on the teacher's professional competence and charisma. The parent was impressed by the initial ability to play a few tunes and may one day be impressed by the child's ability to perform a piece of real music, but all this middle stage seems endless and unsatisfying to them – but not to the child.

These baffled parents ask me: "What sort of child will succeed (in getting to the top of the second ladder)?"

They are surprised to hear that, in my view, progressing to notional "Grade 5" calls for no deep musicality on the part of the child and that any child who is on the right instrument and has been reasonably well taught can get this far – in the same way that any child can, with application and decent tuition, collect a few CSE passes or 'O' levels.

This process of learning may impart something of music to the children, but it does not require them to be innately "musical".

Apart from any friend who may be at the same stage of learning – and such friends are very valuable – the most important person in the child's musical world is his teacher.

The teacher/pupil relationship

The teacher at this stage has three functions: he has to structure and execute a logical progression of learning, he has to provide a continuing source of motivation for the child to pull himself from one rung to the next, and he is the child's audience.

The parents who were excited at the first few simple tunes can find little new to say at the unending succession of exercises and pieces, but the child has worked at each one and requires an audience to perform to. Only the teacher knows what to say, so he becomes the entire audience – with all that that implies.

Not only are parents excluded by a lack of specific knowledge from this new world which the child shares with his teacher, but they, the parents, are often worried at the intensity of the relationship which builds up.

The teacher's importance to the child is not strictly musical. A preschool child relates to very few adults, all within the family situation. At nursery school, the child learns to relate to *one* other adult. "My teacher" replaces "Mummy".

The child on the second ladder is being taught by numerous adults in school and having to share even a favourite teacher with many other children in the class. The relationship with his music teacher is probably the only one-to-one relationship with an adult which the child is able to form outside the family. At the same time, the child/parent bond is being weakened in a number of ways, inevitably and necessarily, as a part of growing up.

Yet, a yearning for personal devotion to an adult is instinctive in young children and there is no harm in the music teacher's harnessing it to the ends of the learning process. Indeed, it is a basic weakness of in-class instrumental teaching that there is no one-to-one relationship and therefore this powerful source of learning-energy is not available.

Because teaching is not simply a mechanical process, every good teacher has his or her own way of continuing the motivation of children who are learning. These include straight bribes: sweets to small children, books and new music to older children.

Teachers can also utilise the natural competitiveness of children who enjoy entering festivals and competitions, providing these are kept free from extrinsic and counter-productive stresses, like parental anxiety and media exposure. (Most teachers can discern for themselves whether parents will pressure a child harmfully and act accordingly.)

Because the teacher/pupil relationship at this stage becomes so exclusive on the child's side, many children get extremely jealous of other pupils going to "my teacher". (In the same way, adults talk of "my doctor", "my analyst"). Many teachers deliberately allow their pupils to hear each other, so that the less good become jealous of those who appear to be making more progress and apply themselves better.

Whilst the teacher is the hero figure, the child gradually becomes aware that his own part of the relationship is less childlike and more mature. It's almost as though the teacher and the pupil were going around in a cheerful and friendly way discovering new challenges *together*. It just happens that the teacher is able to guide the child in the proper direction to surmount each challenge.

Almost imperceptibly, the child begins to absorb the language as well as the grammar of music and becomes aware that he can hold an intelligent conversation, using musical terms naturally and without having to translate at every stage.

Teachers who are happy in their work enjoy the second ladder tremendously and get a great deal from their relationships with pupils, absorbing knowledge and often receiving fresh insight into old and familiar concepts. It is sometimes difficult for teachers who give lesson after lesson, day after day, to remember that, for the child, the lesson is the high-spot and climax of the week's work. The best teachers are those who remember a thousand small quirks and identity components about each child. Young teachers who don't have this gift might make notes on these lines (as much as on the details of learning and progress) and thus ensure that each pupil feels "special".

And where does all this leave the parents?

Parental support

Parents have to learn that the pupil/teacher relationship is the vital one.

The parent's role is to provide support: in other words, to be available when turned to for general encouragement or for specific help in small practical things.

Parents may have to transport the child to and from lessons. This is a mixed blessing. Wherever possible and practicable, I recommend that children should travel to the teacher independently because much mental preparation is necessary before a lesson on the second ladder. After the lesson, a child needs the privacy of his own thoughts to digest all that has been taking place.

Parents can appreciate this, but they find it harder to understand that the child is *performing* for the teacher. Any performer needs to "rev up" before playing and to come down to earth gradually after the performance. A kindly enquiring parent can be very intrusive and actually reduce the overall effect of the time spent with the teacher.

Many children seem to their parents to take an unnecessarily long time returning home after lessons. A couple of bus rides which normally take half an hour can take two or three times as long because the child is apparently dreaming, misses connections, takes too long to walk between two bus stops, and so on. This is natural and good and positive, and indeed many children tack on a post-lesson visit to a music shop or go browsing around looking in shop windows at instruments, visiting the library, and so on. These are all aspects of coming back from the lesson which should be encouraged. Of course, if the child has to rush straight from school to a lesson and come home straight after the lesson because he's too young to be out after dark, there's nothing much that can be done about it, but the parents should still remember that the child is in a condition of mental and emotional exhaustion *if the lesson has been a good one.*

The only contradiction to this policy of parental holding-back is for children learning string instruments. A child learning violin or 'cello needs the weekly lesson to be reinforced day by day and this can only be done by a parent. This specific parental support can be very exacting, particularly for non-musical parents. The sympathetic teacher may encourage parents to make a rough cassette recording of the lesson and use this as a reiteration and point of reference throughout the coming week. Beginner string players may simply be unable to hear what they should be playing and an easy-to-replay cassette can solve many problems, and make progress less agonising and more assured.

It is regarded as normal for parents of very young children to seek out "friends to play with", but, as children grow up, they prefer to find their own friends. However, parents can help a great deal by encouraging the learning child to find situations where he can play with others.

Playing with others

There are two possibilities: playing for fun at home without supervision and playing under supervision in organised groups.

It may be asking a lot to suffer half a dozen brass instruments blown by lusty children or a young rock trio in a modern home, but the more relevant music becomes to the rest of a child's life, the better.

Most of the early instruction books – and the *A Tune A Day* series is particularly good about this – have simple duets and trios which children (between Grades 1 and 5) and their friends can happily cope with, unsupervised.

Even musical parents may have difficulty in appreciating exactly what the child gets from having a tea party with some of his other friends at more or less the same level of attainment and endlessly playing "Merrily we roll along", but a few parallels are useful. Nobody would think that a child had wasted time kicking a football around with some friends for half an hour or that a group visit to the swimming-pool was a waste of time. The essential thing to bear in mind is that, apart from the solo instruments, like the piano and the guitar, music is *all* about playing together with other people. No single-note instrument can justify its existence except together with other instruments.

The sooner children get used to the idea of playing together with others, with the degree of listening and responding which this involves, the easier it is for them to adapt to their first ensemble situations. The playing together for fun is an important *remotivating technique* which is too little exploited. Most children prefer to share any activity together with other children and get a positive enjoyment from the togetherness. In this situation each of the children involved provides a critical audience for the others and is also a part of the all-important peer-group environment.

Also, whilst on the second ladder, children begin to form long-term friendships based on common interests. A common interest in music, whether or not on the same instrument, and a sharing of progress form a powerful bond. Children in non-musical homes actually need to be able to talk about music with someone between lessons.

It is, of course, quite possible that children can adopt bad habits from each other, but these are correctable at the regular weekly lessons by the teacher and the risk is a small price to pay for the potential improvement to be derived from playing together with others.

Children living in rural areas may find that playing together with a few friends informally is the only chance they have of playing with others, but in most towns it is possible to find opportunities in supervised situations. There are Saturday-morning orchestras, junior brass bands, wind bands and Music Centres organised and run by peripatetic teachers as part of their working week. Some schools have excellent orchestras organised and conducted by the music teacher.

Where these groups are organised within the educational system, they may discriminate against children who are learning privately and particularly virulently against children on modern, electric instruments.

It is sadly a matter of luck and chance what exists in your area. If you live in Commuterville with middle-class schools, you stand a fair chance. If you live in a depressed part of the country or far from a centre of population, your children are at a disadvantage in this respect, as in so many others.

Some junior orchestras are run for the benefit of the very few really talented children in the community, with the others being accepted just to make the numbers up. Yet, the true point and aim of all these orchestras is the enjoyment which *all* children who are learning can exact from this situation, by contributing their part to the musical whole.

Conducting orchestras made up of maybe a hundred excited children trying to play their best in front of the others and the conductor and any teachers who may be there, is a demanding and exhausting job which requires a particular talent and personality. Parents who may misguidedly hang around to see what is going on will probably understand very little and just conclude that the children are making an awful din and that the teacher/conductor is wasting his time. However apparently unmusical the result, children get far more from these activities than their parents can guess.

Going *en masse* with the rest of the Saturday-morning orchestra to perform at a festival or competition, or to give a concert in the local works canteen or for the pensioners, can be an exhilarating and rewarding experience for children on the second ladder.

On the other hand, joining one of these little orchestras or groups can be shattering. Children who were apparently making good progress may suddenly give up when they discover – through the exigencies of playing together with others under a conductor – that they cannot sight-read, that they cannot pitch a note, that they cannot understand rhythm. These children are forced to realise that learning by rote is one thing; coming to understand music is something else.

Parents who find that a child becomes dispirited and demoralised after joining an orchestra should think seriously about the dual question: "Is the teacher/instrument the right one for my child?"

Apart from the enjoyment they afford, this make-or-break function alone would justify the existence of all these junior orchestras and bands.

The contemporary headache for teachers and others organising these groups is the imbalance in the number of children learning different instruments. Traditionally, the ratio was one woodwind-player to about five or ten string-players. Look at any orchestra and see what I mean. Today, the ratios are inverted. Because so many children start on the recorder and because so many parents and teachers assume that progress on the recorder reveals a talent for woodwind, we are inundated by young flautists and clarinettists.

Conversely, it is a desperate search to find enough children who want to undertake the hard slog of the string instruments.

This situation can land the conductor in front of a junior orchestra composed of:

20 flutes
25 clarinets
1 alto saxophone
2 bassoons
1 oboe
4 cornets
1 trumpet
1 trombone
8 violins
1 'cello

with, waiting, willing, but unwanted: two electric guitarists who can read music and three drumkit-players who can't.

It is difficult to find repertoire to play for such combinations but, until we musicians and music teachers have remedied the imbalance, it is unfair of us to discourage children. If there are forty flutes and no fiddles, we must start flute bands. If we are about to be overrun by hordes of clarinettists, we must provide them with multi-part arrangements for clarinet choirs.

At the Bentovim Day Schools, we frequently cope with such combinations of instruments and play specially written arrangements* of classical, folk and pop music with tremendous success.

It doesn't matter what the spectators and parents make of it all, the point is that the children enjoy what they are doing, derive the normal and natural benefits of playing with others and – very important – nobody feels left out.

At this stage, children are not capable of making true music; they are involved in a learning process. To quibble about the balance or musical logic of such groups playing together is to delude oneself about the reason why the children are playing their instruments at this stage of development.

"What else can I play?"

For most instruments, the basic repertoire which has to be mastered in

* Now being published by Novello & Co. under the title "Atarah's Band Kits".

order to pass exams hasn't changed much since I was a child a quarter of a century ago.

In those days, children didn't have television or transistor radios, and music was something which happened once a week at school. For me, in any case, there was a lot of point in gaining an extensive repertoire of classical music, since it was assumed from the first moment I touched a flute that I should grow up to be a professional musician.

However, today, and particularly for the children about whom this book is written, an almost exclusive diet of classical music, leavened here and there with a folk melody, is disaster. Most children who are learning instruments and are on the second ladder live in a world where classical music is never normally heard except as the signature tune of a television series. Arts administrators, musicians and teachers may wishfully delude themselves, but classical music is dead as far as most children are concerned.

A child on the second ladder learning a Mozart minuet or a Little Prelude by Bach is not coming to a wonderful understanding of Bach and Mozart; he is doing an exercise which the teacher has set that week. This is no more or less than the way in which his class at school may be reading Hamlet. They are not gaining a true insight into the literary genius of Shakespeare; they're slogging away for an exam at the end of term.

Some teachers are very good at extending a child's informal repertoire by finding simple arrangements of recent pop and light music of which a growing number is coming on to the market. Parents can help a lot here, by taking a child to browse round the sheet music and albums in the local music shop to find theme music for a film the child has enjoyed or a tune associated with a popular television programme. Musicians automatically browse through music shops in the same way as other people look through the contents of a station bookstall, but non-musical parents have to think consciously about inculcating this rewarding habit in their children.

Children will want to save pocket money if they find simple music which is interesting to play and, once having bought it, will work very hard at mastering the piece well enough to play to someone.

Children who play in organised groups may be better looked after than the rest. Junior sections of brass bands usually have many easy arrangements of current pop hits and light music. Energetic individual music teachers and conductors of youth orchestras often spend long hours arranging simple versions of children's favourites –

and copying out all the parts – to find that the children enjoy playing these far more than the outdated repertoire available off the shelf.

Practising

The child who still has to think about whether or not he wants to practise is almost bound to fall off the second ladder.

The child who learned to practise regularly and routinely on the first ladder has no problems now. For him, all that is necessary is gradually to build up the amount of time spent on the instrument each day, in order to learn the longer and more difficult pieces of music and to improve speed, technique and quality of sound.

It's important for parents to realise that he does have to increase the time allowed for practice. If he practises five minutes a day, he'll be travelling backwards. Ten minutes a day will keep him marking time. With thirty or forty minutes a day, he will forge ahead.

Children at this stage who practise more than a good forty minutes or so a day are – unless very talented – more likely to be doing it in order to relieve other frustrations and pressures than in order to improve. Excessive "practising" tends not to develop the child so much as to reconfirm him in his own bad habits.

Now and again, even the best learner has a bad phase and can't see the point of practising, or resents what seems to be an encroachment upon his own free time. Parents are faced with the dilemma of whether or not to force the child to practise. Sometimes an oblique approach is best, with the parent finding a new, albeit temporary, motivation by taking the child to an evening concert, by finding some supervised or informal group to play with or even just by purchasing – with help and advice from the shop assistant – an unexpected present of some new music to play.

Some teachers have a great deal of success by treating this unwillingness to practise as an indication that the child is insufficiently stretched and recommend, as an answer, starting the pupil on a second instrument as well as, not instead of, the first study. In this way, children who have been feeling a bit stale on the flute or clarinet may be encouraged to try a more difficult instrument such as the piano or guitar which will help to make sense of the theory they have learned. Children on a more difficult instrument like the guitar or violin will find the flute or clarinet almost a push-over.

In either case, the excitement of the new instrument almost always has a beneficial effect on the first study.

If inducements of this kind do not do the trick, it's worth the parent examining whether the child is on the right instrument, or whether his unwillingness to practise is rooted in the insecurity that comes from having skimped some of the essential learning, which leaves the child unable to work without the presence and support of the teacher.

Essential learning

On the first ladder, the pupil had to work blindly for the teacher. If the teacher said it was necessary to concentrate on a particular aspect of theory or to practise a particular piece of music as an exercise, the reason for the child to do the work was simply because "teacher said so".

On the second ladder, this blind obedience becomes increasingly less requisite as the pupil himself begins to relate the various areas of study. The first time he tries to write out a simple piece of music for himself and some friends to play, he will start to realise why it is necessary to study theory. The first time he tries to strum along with a pop record, he will understand the reason for aural training! The first session in a junior orchestra, confronted by a piece of music he hasn't seen before will convince him the teacher was right to insist on sight-reading exercises. In criticising a friend's performance on the same instrument, he will come to listen more critically to the quality of his own sound. When he finds other children able to play faster and more precisely, he will realise the importance of attention to technique.

The essential learning which has to be imparted by the teacher is a continuation of the several bases established on the first ladder. The difference is that the child comes to derive more and more of the motivation to learn from external stimuli.

One of the functions of examinations – several of which are encountered on the second ladder – is that they afford child, parent and teacher alike the opportunity of checking that the child is receiving a balanced course of study in all aspects of music. For those who don't already know, the essential elements in an Associated Board's instrumental performance examination are:

> performance of short set pieces;
> performance of a study involving a technical problem;
> selected scales;
> reasonably difficult aural tests;
> a sight-reading exercise.

Parents who find from the helpfully laid-out examination result form that the child is gaining high marks for performance (which is what he most enjoys) but very low marks for aural training or sight-reading should have a little chat with the teacher!

Conclusion

For most children, arriving at the top of the second ladder will coincide with "dropping subjects" at school. Some children will decide that they want to stop their instrumental studies in the same way that they opt out of geography or art and there should be no disgrace in this, for they have already demonstrated a considerable achievement. In any case, a child who drops geography does not forget North and South or the outline of the map of England, so the child who drops music does not lose everything which he has so laboriously acquired.

By this stage, any child is well equipped to take an intelligent interest in listening to music, to take up playing in a folk group or jazz band or brass band – for *fun*. A child at the top of the ladder with Grade 5 on piano or classical guitar will happily be able to be a star feature of the school concert. On the light music instruments, someone with this high degree of musical education would be an invaluable asset to many a pop group!

Some children may step almost unconsciously from the first ladder on to the second, but few will be unaware of the transition from the top of the second ladder on to the first rungs of the third. It is at this stage that the Associated Board insists on a separate theory examination. The child is approaching the stage where he faces not simplified arrangements but real music as written by the composer. And there's no mistaking the difference!

The third ladder is hard work.

Section 11
The Third Ladder: Making It to Notional Grade 8

"By the time the pupil gets to the top of the third ladder, he is able to make true music – not in the sense of becoming a professional performer, but with the instrument so much within his grasp, the theory of music so absorbed, that he can take a full part in amateur music-making and think of taking up a career which requires a peripheral knowledge of music.

"This is somewhere about the level of the Associated Board's Grade 8 examination or the performing part of GCE 'A' level."

In many ways the attainment of Grade 5 is the end of musical childhood and the beginning of musical adolescence. Everything changes: a pupil's own attitude to music, the teacher/pupil relationship, the essential quality of the music which is being studied and performed . . .

On the first two ladders, the pupil played either simplified arrangements or simple pieces selected from the repertoire for his instrument. In either case, he was using the pieces as exercises in order to improve technique and aid mastery of the instrument.

On the third ladder, he is finished with simplified arrangements and has to grapple with no-compromise writing: he has to play compositions as required by the composer, who was not writing a technical exercise, but a piece of *music*.

This is an abrupt and sometimes humiliating transition. The pupil on the earlier ladders has only himself and perhaps a friend to listen to. At the best, he can just recall how the teacher demonstrated the piece. Now, he is confronted on record and cassette, on radio and on television, with the sound of the world's greatest musicians playing the same pieces of music which he, the pupil, is studying. It is impossible for him to be unaware of the vast gap between the standards of these professionals and himself. This is a frightening demonstration of the distance still to travel.

It can take a great deal of confidence, courage and perseverance for a child to keep going.

Paradoxically, once young people have definitely started on the third ladder, they are unlikely to fall off it.

A talented 15-year-old violinist, nearly at the top of the third ladder, recording for a Radio City "Atarah's Bandstand" programme

Given a more or less constant level of musical ability, students can travel up the first and second ladder at greatly differing speeds: woodwind players move very fast while violinists, pianists and guitarists progress almost imperceptibly (except to their teachers). On the third ladder, there is a kind of levelling out, for the work which has to be done has as much to do with the child's developing intellect and sense of music as with the technical problems of the instrument. On whichever instrument, climbing up the third ladder normally takes two or three years of sustained hard work.

The teacher/pupil relationship

The job of a teacher is to make himself dispensable.

Parents and teachers alike should be aware that, when a child on the third ladder wants to leave the teacher who has earlier been a hero figure and source of inspiration, this is not a betrayal, but simply a gesture of maturescence on the part of the pupil who recognises instinctively that he needs a teacher with something different to offer.

Some music teachers may be ideally suited to dealing very creatively with young children and yet be unable to cope with adolescent assertions of personality which may seem to them aggressive and hostile, although they are simply an inevitable part of growing up, both personally and musically.

Others who may be ideal for older children on the third ladder may be hopeless at giving younger children the basic grounding in music. In schools, the same teacher does not handle both nursery children and the Sixth Form, after all . . .

Because the learning process is taking place while a child's whole being is changing and developing from that of a physically weak, dependent and inexperienced creature to that of an almost independent adult, some of the crises in the teacher/pupil relationship are really externalisations of the crises in the parent/child relationship.

Teachers who regard the stimulating relationships with older pupils as part of their reward for coping with the musically unsatisfying earlier stages, often find themselves fighting a pupil's desire to leave them and trying to enlist the parents in the fight against the child's decision. This is a hopeless and unrewarding situation paralleled by that of parents who try to stop their children growing up and becoming independent.

Sometimes, a pupil may appear dissatisfied with his teacher when what he really seeks is a new pattern of tuition: he no longer needs the regular weekly reinforcement of discipline, but he does need more time at each lesson to go more fully into the technical and creative problems which arise at this stage. In such a case, the solution may be to abandon the system of short weekly lessons in favour of longer lessons at intervals of two or three weeks.

Some pupils find a strong inclination to do away with regular lessons from a teacher altogether and have irregular sessions with a performing musician.

A compromise which can work if there is no real possibility of finding another teacher within reasonable travelling distance is to stay with the teacher for the regular lessons but to have, now and again, an inspirational session with an admired performer.

If parents find that the child is still basically dissatisfied with the teacher, they must harden their hearts and somehow find a new one. A teacher/pupil relationship which has been outgrown is sterile and in the end destructive – certainly for the pupil and probably for the teacher.

Even if he stays with the same teacher, the child on the third ladder becomes less and less able to accept the teacher's dicta. Pupils – particularly as they approach Grade 8 – may become almost hostile and very destructive about particular aspects of a teacher's technique or style of playing. And the child has a point: if the teacher is simply a teacher and has never been a performer, who is to say which is right? Teachers who are also performers have this a little easier, for, after all, if the rest of an orchestra, the public and the critics like the teacher's style and sound, the child will feel less able to "rip him to bits". But, still, he will often try.

The irony is that it is the teacher who has equipped the child to make this kind of critical judgement. If he hadn't, he would have been failing in his duty as a teacher ...

Once a decision to find a new teacher has been made, the easier the break, the better for the child. Many keep in touch with their first music teacher for years after leaving him and, as they grow older, use him as a guide and mentor in ways which have little to do with music, thus demonstrating affection and gratitude which had previously conflicted with the need for a new kind of teaching.

Apart from musical reasons for leaving a teacher, there are emotional ones. Parents should be on their guard, for a child expressing too intense a desire either to stay with a teacher or to leave a teacher may be influenced by the very normal adolescent phenomenon of falling in love with an admired adult of either sex. Because of the intensity of the teacher/pupil relationship at this stage, because it is a one-to-one relationship and because lessons have to be conducted in privacy, it is often very hard for teachers, particularly young ones, to handle the emotional side.

The teacher who is right for a child at this stage of musical development will be uncompromising as to technique, quality of sound and interpretation. He will be ruthless in attacking bad habits in the fields of technique and physical attitude to the instrument which will otherwise be set for life.

This is the reason why many parents think that a new teacher has been a disastrous mistake. The pupil abruptly stops making any progress and appears to be shattered psychologically and musically as the teacher dismantles the whole conscious and subconscious process of playing – in order to reassemble it correctly.

Instead of moving on to exciting new pieces, a young wind-player may be restricted for several weeks to practising for two hours a day blowing sustained notes in order to correct an embouchure fault. A string-player may be set to playing open strings in order to correct bowing technique. A guitarist may be put back to playing scales in order to correct a left-hand defect.

Doing this in order to repair basic technique is one thing, but teachers should beware of carrying out such major surgery merely to impose their own methods, or those of a particular style or school of playing, on children who have a reasonable technique but are seeking to express their own personality (perfectly legitimate at this stage) which may be very different from that of the teacher.

It is important for both the parent and the new teacher to be very honest with themselves and the child. If a teacher basically dislikes the kind of sound which a child is making, yet cannot fault his basic technique, it is only fair to refuse to teach that child, rather than run the risk of destroying the child's confidence and musical identity.

This book is not about talented children. Yet, this is a dangerous moment for them, too. They almost all leave their teacher-teacher at this stage and come into contact with a performer-teacher. On the one hand, a performer-teacher has all the experience to guide them towards a professional playing career, but on the other hand, he may have a deeply-rooted subconscious antagonism towards tomorrow's players who will eventually replace him on the concert platform.

This may drive him to attack the very roots of the young player's musical identity with profound results which may take many years to overcome.

There are other schools of thought, but my personal belief, based upon results, is that the best teachers to help most pupils up the third ladder are musicians who have done a certain amount of performing but are now happy to concentrate on the delightful role of bringing forward the next generation.

For teachers of average children, this is an uneasy but very reward-ing time. There is a considerable impetus within the child to extend repertoire, to improve technique, to increase musical knowledge, but this is never enough and the necessary progress will only be accomplished by the teacher "pushing" the pupil from one achievement to the next, constantly criticising yet stimulating.

This is the stage at which woodwind students should begin to tackle the orchestral repertoire, pianists should be persuaded to accompany, classical brass-players should be forced to cope with the problems of swinging light music, and guitarists should be made to perform in public and exposed to sight-reading situations.

If the third ladder is hard work for the pupil, parents should be aware that it is also unrelenting hard work for the teacher!

Parental support

Parental support at this stage can be painful – in the direction of the bank account!

Children who have been learning on a good second-hand instrument may be able to continue without changing, but almost every child who has been learning on a student instrument will need to change to a better quality one.

Whereas, to begin with, many parents are understandably reluctant to over-invest in a musical instrument, the child who has pursued a course of study as far as this is unlikely to abandon the instrument for many years. It will almost certainly appreciate in value as the years go by. If anything, the best advice is to spend more money than the minimum necessary to get a better instrument, in the hope that the one now purchased will last the child for life. It would be marvellous if you could buy cars or domestic machines which were as durable!

The cost of lessons may increase radically. Even students who stay with the same teacher may find that they need an hour a week instead of thirty minutes. Students transferring from a teacher-teacher to a performer-teacher may have to pay two or three times as much for the same amount of tuition time.

Children – particularly those who don't live in a major town – have to do a lot of travelling for lessons, to attend concerts, to take part in festivals and competitions, or to play in youth orchestras.

Where free in-school lessons have previously been available, the parents may be taken aback at the cost of private one-to-one lessons necessary to progress further. Bear in mind that it is always worth finding out about Studentship schemes, and asking generally for assistance from the educational system towards the cost of taking lessons, travelling and purchase of music, especially when the child is taking music as part of GCE or CSE examinations for which he has been entered by the school.

There are holiday courses, weekend courses, junior master classes, all of which cost money, but fees and travelling expenses for these do not necessarily have to come out of the parent's pocket. All my holiday courses were paid for out of the proceeds of my own teaching.

Children on the third ladder, with the right personality, should be encouraged to start giving lessons to beginners. Young people have an *instinct to give* which is so often repressed, yet here is a golden opportunity to help younger children and make a little income. Fees charged should be kept modest, but the lessons should not be free. The child learning music is kept dependent on the parent in so many ways that helping him to obtain some legitimate private income is a very healthy thing to do.

Parental know-how can be a boon. Perhaps few teenagers would think of buying an advert in the local paper or writing out half a dozen postcards to go in shop windows, but any parent can do that, advertising the young player's ability and willingness to give lessons to beginners. The mother of one young guitarist whom I interviewed for my Radio 3 series found that a single postcard in the local sweet-shop window brought three pupils in the first week. At one stroke, she had solved her son's need for some independent income and the problem of other sets of parents who had been looking for local tuition for months.

The parental role is not, on balance, a painful one. The musical ability and progress of the child is now becoming apparent even to the least musical parent and this is an exciting thing to watch developing. Also, an adolescent with a serious interest in music is almost always easier to live with than one with no focus or creative outlet for all the restless energy of this time of life!

Moreover, the child who has earlier excluded non-musical parents from the musical side of his life will now begin to want someone to talk to. This is interesting because many children at this stage "clam up" and do not tell their parents anything. For some reason, music can be the one subject which is not too private and embarrassing to talk about with one's parents.

One surprising duty for parents is to watch that their children do not practise too much.

Practising

The healthy approach to practice is for the child to plan a regular pattern of activities, allotting, in order of personal preferences, separate periods of time for basic technique, scales, studies and, lastly,

A shared interest in music. Electric guitars join with classical instruments at a Bentovim Day School

repertoire. Most children have plenty of other things to do with their "spare" time. Conflicting demands can make them very unclear as to priorities and the best way of using practice time. When in doubt, concentrate on basic technique – and repertoire will follow. Concentrating on repertoire to the detriment of technique may be more fun at the time, but slows down progress.

A simple rule is that three periods of twenty minutes each, or two half-hours, are far better, healthier, more productive and less exhausting than a neurotic and shattering two- or three-hour long battle with the instrument.

Adolescents may indulge in excessive practising for non-musical reasons, especially to avoid dwelling on troubling sexual problems. The ritual and peacefulness of practice can be a haven amid the turmoil of awakening sexuality. Within reasonable limits, being able to retreat into the privacy of practice is one of the benefits of the third ladder.

Excessive practising for musical reasons is what parents have to be on the look-out for. The child is now old enough and sufficiently experienced musically to know how much work *could* still be done on the instrument. This can lead to a panic situation of trying to crowd more and more practising into each day of the week, in the conviction that giving up every reasonable pleasure somehow attracts musical merit in compensation. It doesn't work that way.

Repertoire

The young player on the third ladder finds his repertoire extending almost rung by rung until, by the time he reaches the top, much of the music ever written for his instrument lies literally at his fingertips. This is not to say that he is good enough to perform in public for the enjoyment of others, but he is good enough to play a wonderful spread of music for his own pleasure.

Unfortunately, virtually all the repertoire required for examination, festival or competition purposes is still drawn from the classical world. However, the learner is by now educated to discern the musical validity of the selected pieces. They may still seem boring and uninspiring to the non-musical parent listening, but they are not so to the player.

Playing with others

The possibilities for making music, whether supervised or unsupervised, together with coevals and other amateur musicians of all ages are now limited only by the personal tastes of the young player. Teachers and parents, far from trying to perpetuate their own prejudices on the next generation, should try to encourage every young player to explore new fields of music. The classically trained should learn to improvise; the dance band trumpeter should get to know Purcell.

The aim should be to explore all music and find the kind which best suits the young player's personality and will continue to give him playing satisfaction and pleasure long after all the hard work of learning has been forgotten.

It doesn't matter whether he wants to freak out in jazz or pop vein against the throb of a twelve-bar blues backing, join a string quartet or form a wind quintet. Never before has it been so easy for an amateur musician to find, and do, "his own thing". This is a remarkable freedom which non-musical parents cannot appreciate. Children who don't make it up the third ladder never quite get to this plateau.

The young musician with a genuine interest in rock or pop music now finds that he is very much sought after by musically-uneducated coevals who are still fumbling to improve technique on their own, to gain a little bit of musical theory, to learn to play together. He is in the position of a natural leader, able to take a number of young players who could never get together on their own and blend them into a group. He alone can write simple arrangements, solve the musical problems which constantly frustrate them and keep the group in time and in tune!

Many adolescents find it difficult to make friends outside the immediate school environment. A shared interest in music, particularly attendance at holiday and weekend courses, or playing in

Atarah with young players during a group improvisation session at a Bentovim Day School

a youth orchestra, is a powerful way of breaking the ice and a lot better than the inadequate attempts at conversation of adolescents who have nothing in common.

Conflict with other studies and interests

The spare time of youth has to be stretched in three directions to cope with homework and musical activities, but also to leave a reasonable amount of time to meet boy- and girl-friends and generally learn how to behave in society.

It's true that there is a lot of work to be done on the third ladder, but at the same time there is a lot of work to be done at school and it is also important that the adolescent's social development should not be neglected.

It is one of the great sadnesses of exceptionally talented children that the amount of time which they are forced to devote to music almost always deprives them of a healthy and enjoyable adolescence. Not only is this unfair at the time, but it leads to many unhappy marriages and mismanaged lives for the simple reason that they never had the chance to develop as adults during the period when Nature intended: adolescence.

Putting music into perspective

It is *so* difficult for any parent – whether musically educated or not – to know how good his or her child is. It can be a torment, wondering whether to switch from a gently supporting role to a position of applying pressure on the child "to take music more seriously". One of the healthiest functions of festivals and competitions is to let parents hear their children play in direct comparison with others.

I receive many letters from parents asking how they can pressure their children into thinking of a musical career. Many intelligent and cultured parents come to think in these terms as soon as their child demonstrates a reasonable fluency on the instrument. I have had such letters from parents of three-year-olds who have played two notes on a plastic recorder, and even one written request for help from the mother of an eighteen-month-old toddler who enjoyed clapping to the music on the radio!

As a piece of general advice, it is almost certain that a child with talent who should be pressured in this way will have been singled out for special treatment by the teacher, or someone at school, leaving the parents in no doubt.

It is important to keep music in perspective and view the results which can be obtained by hard work in much the same way as achievements on the football or athletic field. Few people would seriously tell a good young footballer or athlete to envisage a career as a professional sportsman. Treat music the same way, for the odds of making a career out of it are no better.

Conclusion

The young player may be the last person to realise it – for the young do not think of old or even middle age – but he has now gained a hobby and absorbing leisure interest which can occupy as little or as much leisure time as he may have throughout his life. Unlike his sporting friends, there is no need for him to abandon his one great interest by his thirtieth birthday and thereafter only watch other people doing it on television. Many amateur musicians find that their pleasure in music increases as the years go by.

Even if our young player were to discard his instrument the day after passing Grade 8, he has already been amply repaid for all his hard work, by never having been at a loss for "something to do", by the knowledge that he has achieved a great deal largely through his own self-discipline, by the balanced development of mental, physical and spiritual co-ordination and by the therapy which music has already afforded him through some of the trials and more difficult periods of growing up.

He is immensely richer than his coevals who have not followed a course of instrumental learning, because he is equipped to enjoy music both actively and passively and this is his lifelong gift.

It takes a lot of hard work – by child, parent and teachers – but it's worth it.

Atarah telling a musical story

A working session in a comprehensive school gym

Appendix 1
How I Became Involved

Inspiration, as we have seen, may not be easy to come by.

I was lucky enough to get mine in the home. My father, a London GP, must have fancied himself as one of the early disc jockeys, and filled the home, the waiting-rooms, the halls and stairways with the sound of classical records from his extensive collection of 78's. As a boy in Jerusalem, he had learned to play the violin. His mother traded vegetables, which were scarce there during the First World War, for violin lessons from a temperamental (and presumably hungry) Russian professor of music. Although Father never touched the violin after the age of sixteen, this early grounding in music was never lost.

A generation later, the home in which I grew up was full of music, both classical and light. All my brothers played musical instruments, my mother was an avid opera fan, and both my parents went regularly to concerts. For me, there was never any question of music being accessible. It was all round us, every day.

Most classical musicians have had a similar, if perhaps less exotic background, which is why they find it hard to understand what it is like for children from homes where music consists solely of pop on radio and television. The very people who are technically able to devise new approaches to music for modern children cannot see the necessity to do so, because they themselves had no such need.

Why, therefore, did I take an interest in this field?

After all, I had the conventional childhood and adolescence of a musical prodigy, playing my first concerto on television with the Royal Philharmonic Orchestra at the age of sixteen and was Principal Flute at a prom in the Royal Albert Hall the following year. At the Royal Academy of Music, I studied with a remarkable and highly talented generation of musicians. The French Government gave me a scholarship to study in France.

Before I was twenty-two, I had played Principal Flute with Ballet Rambert and at Sadlers Wells. The same year – exceptionally young for the job, I beat James Galway to the post of Principal Flute with the Royal Liverpool Philharmonic Orchestra. I could not have had a more wonderfully ecstatic and fulfilling start to my musical career.

From the time I was fourteen I had been teaching privately, with over forty pupils by my eighteenth birthday. It was this contact with other young people from all backgrounds and not all of whom shared my fanatical love for classical music which first led me to suspect that there might be such a thing as the Musical Obstacle Race.

As a performer, amid all the fulfilment of my music-making the only adverse moments were when I played at schools' concerts and family concerts and perceived the abyss between those of us who appreciated music and the average modern, media-educated child. Conductor after conductor bored thousands of children with an inappropriate choice of music and with no idea how to contact musically-uneducated youngsters. I felt that we all, conductors, musicians and managements, were cheating the children out of what they had a right to expect. My fellow musicians were mostly passive people who responded to my tirades about this by saying, more or less: "Why don't *you* do something about it?".

My dilemma was that, as an individual I could have no influence upon the educational system, the lack of guidance available in the community, the lack of facilities. These were problems only politicians could tackle.

There was little I could do about radio and television programmes, but I tried. "They", the programme makers, all said more or less: "Come back when you're famous and we'll make you more famous." The record companies were deaf to everything except the sound of cash registers.

But, I felt, surely I could do something about the most important source of inspiration, of which I did know something: live music.

So I did. I went to orchestral managements and tried to convince them to do something more imaginative and more likely to engage the attention of children, on the grounds that flying paper aeroplanes off the balcony was their way of telling us that we weren't coming up to their expectations. After a few polite brush-offs, I realised that I was coming to be regarded as just another crazy woman with a bee in her bonnet.

So I started to promote my own concerts, experimenting with every possible ensemble from two to twenty-two musicians. Out of my meagre pay, I found their meagre fees, booked halls, paid for advertising and printing tickets, and stood in the foyer after concerts giving out handbills to anyone who looked as if he or she might have children to bring. A major problem was the lack of exciting repertoire, so I asked composers and arrangers whom I knew to write new material. (If they'd all wanted proper fees for those first few concerts, we'd never have got started).

There was never any subsidy available for these exercises. One of the marvellous things about not having a subsidy is that it teaches you very fast not to make the same mistake twice.

And people came!

Appendix 2
One Way to Improve Children's Concerts–The Atarah's Band Approach

After some years of experimenting with a few talented, forbearing friends, I formed a partnership with – and subsequently married – a Television Producer who had experience of producing just about every kind of entertainment from circuses to chamber music, and with a background in children's films. He confessed to knowing nothing about music, which seemed an advantage, because I had lots of friends who knew about music. What I needed was someone who knew about contacting audiences.

At first this was, to him, just another production job. Musicians are so obsessed with their music that they all tend to forget about the audience. It was an eye-opener to find someone who *began* by finding out what the audience was and what it needed, and then started to think about the format of concert which might work.

It was obvious that we couldn't just wander on to the platform, sit down and play movements of existing repertoire lasting ten or fifteen minutes each. Our Producer explained that a passive audience of children was most likely just day-dreaming as children learn to do during boring lessons at school; that, if we wanted children to get something from the experience of live music, we had to find ways of channelling their natural energy, not suppressing it. He also made the point that standing on the conductor's rostrum and chatting to the audience *about music* was useless. Unless you already understand about music, none of the words of musicologists and critics and music-lovers means anything!

The problem, then, was to find – within the format of an entertainment – sufficient metaphors to explain the essence of the music and the character of the instruments, without using words which the children could not understand. At the same time, we had to make the experience as much fun for the children as going to a concert is for musically-educated adults. And there were no precedents to follow!

We started to build a show, selecting a combination of instruments which would enable us to integrate, within one musical experience, music of all styles and periods from Early Music through arrangements of classical music to modern rock and pop. We built in audience participation, and allowed for the fact that children could not concentrate for more than a couple of minutes without either relief or some special motivation. We drafted quizzes and designed costumes and music-stands. We invented a team of Musical Animals and soldiers and robots and clowns to focus the children's attention on particularly important points. We worked out every last detail of the format, the style of presentation, the aims, the links, even the moves on stage. We found musicians who were virtuosi on their instruments *and* could cope with the rare stress of playing such a diversity of music. As if that wasn't enough to ask of them, they also had to get used to split-second timings of entrances and exits, as important as playing the right notes. (Telly-educated children are distracted by musicians who amble on to the platform chatting about what they had for breakfast and then sit down unnecessarily tuning up for a couple of minutes before they play).

Because every phrase of the music had to be specially written by someone who understood what we were doing, we gave writer's cramp to the small nucleus of composers and arrangers who worked with us.

To free me for the role of presenting the concerts, we looked for and found an exceptional Musical Director, equally at home playing improvised modern jazz or Bach lute music or arrangements of classical music, and with a lightning brain which enables him to take in his stride instant changes of programme.

We discovered that we had to build up three distinct "shows" or styles of presentation: for the under-eights, for eight- to eleven-year-olds and for teenagers, and that evening family shows to which older children came with Mums and Dads needed yet another style again. Each "show" meant starting from scratch and amassing an extensive repertoire of music from which to select our programmes.

We used all the tricks of modern showbusiness and some of our own.

Our aim throughout was to *produce* a music show from which children could get as much entertainment on their own level as adults would expect at evening concerts. In addition, we integrated and disguised a lot of discrete education, to feed children's natural hunger for information, with quizzes, rhythm exercises, participation, demonstrations, sound-recognition and . . . and . . . and . . .

We decided, as a policy, that instead of retiring to the dressing-room at interval-time and after the show, I must be in the audience, walking about and talking freely with the children so that any of them (or their Mums and Dads) could come up to me and chat about music, tell me how they were getting on, ask my advice on problems. We sent them backstage to talk with individual members of the Band for specific advice about instruments.

Thanks to my early experimentation, I had already presented more children's concerts than anyone else. But if I thought that the role of presenter was an easy one, I was in for a shock. Years of training in BBC tv had taught my Producer never to leave anything to chance. So, for hour after hour, I was made to stand in front of a standard lamp, pretending it was a microphone, going over and over every single word of my linking material and being grilled on the meaning of every word – until I could have screamed.

(Even today, whenever we work up a new show, I still have to go through this performer's Third Degree).

I had to learn that only thus can a presenter get to the point of being able to throw away the script – and, if necessary, change the programme which has been rehearsed with the musicians, in order to respond to the reaction of the audience once the show has started. No two audiences of children are the same. Geography, local economics and traditions, racial mixtures, ages, educational standards, familiarity with live entertainment (let alone music) all affect the needs of an audience and only by the presenter controlling and changing the planned programme, as necessary, can the show be kept in full contact with the audience. It doesn't matter what worked last time, the present audience is the only important one.

We had to find a name. Children told us not to use words like:
                    orchestra
                    ensemble
                    symphony
                    classical
                    chamber music
                    concert

and suggested, instead:

                    group
                    "live disco" (whatever that is!)
                    rave-up
                    fun show
                    band
                    music party

They thought that Atarah was a great name, because it "sounds like a rock star" ... and "you don't know if it's a boy or a girl". This market research operation eventually narrowed the short list down to "Atarah's Band". (Atarah is my real name and the only proper generic name for such an elastic group of musicians must be "Band").

My job as Principal Flautist with the R.L.P.O. took up five days a week, in addition to teaching commitments and a lot of chamber music engagements. My husband didn't exactly have a lot of spare time either, being a BBC Staff Television Producer. We had the choice of either carrying on with our present jobs and doing a few children's concerts whenever we could fit them in, or of giving up our exciting and satisfying careers and cutting down on every other kind of commitment to become the first full-time producers, presenters and performers of a new concept in children's concerts, moving from the security of pensions, paid holidays and sick leave to the harsh Victorian reality of the self-employed.

The more we learnt about inspiring children towards music, the more we found we didn't know. Against that, the more we learnt about what wasn't being done elsewhere, the more fuel we acquired to feed the fires of our own fanaticism.

We have done concerts promoted by the Hallé, the Royal Liverpool Philharmonic Society, the Scottish National Orchestra, the City of Birmingham Symphony Orchestra. Festivals came to us, sometimes asking for just one concert, sometimes for highly imaginative programmes of musical activity spread over several days to excite and awaken the children of the area. Leisure Service Officers asked us if it would be possible to have concerts in sports halls. (It was – with a lot of hard work). Arts Associations asked us to take music into situations where it had never succeeded before. Energetic Head Teachers, Music Teachers and Music Advisers took over large halls and filled them for two shows a day – like pantomime – with children who had never been to any live music in their lives.

Lack of subsidy meant that we didn't have to account to anybody for our actions. If we had had to justify each step to committees and wait for budgets to be appropriated, we should never had got started. The only times we regretted our inability to tap public funds were when we were asked to go and work for remote communities or for small audiences which couldn't afford a proper fee.

We found that we were doing about two hundred concerts a year – as many as any long-established, subsidised, properly-managed symphony orchestra – plus a lot of travelling, plus broadcasting work, plus recording sessions. We had to set up our own management company, a record production company, a publishing operation, and make them all financially self-sufficient.

And then we discovered another job waiting for us. Thousands of children who had been to the concerts wanted to take up an instrument and learn to play. Teachers and parents and children wrote and telephoned to ask where they could go for the next stage of choosing the right instrument, getting an instrument, finding a teacher, and so on.

There was no answer, until we realised that we were living in it. Our forty-four rooms of dry rot, wet rot, woodworm and general decay, were ideal for conversion into a children's music centre where children and parents and non-specialist teachers could come for just this kind of help.

We set up the Bentovim Children's Music Centre Trust, converting our premises room by room to provide the first ever musical leisure centre for children.

Hopefully, it won't be too long before the need to inspire children towards music generally is recognised within the cultural community as a legitimate need and one which can be fulfilled by training, allocation of resources, by provision of premises and equipment.

To begin with, we were regarded as cranks. When we began to *do*, instead of just talk, we were looked upon as fanatics. Now, it's nice to be hailed as the first professionals in the field. We hope it won't be too long before we're joined by many more.

143

Appendix 3
"I Can Play..."

Twelve extracts from interviews for the BBC Radio 3 series "Atarah's Music Box".

EXTRACT 1: Michaela, aged 9

        Learning trumpet for three years.
        Grade 5.

        (MUSIC – MICHAELA PLAYS)

Atarah:	Michaela, what was that you just played?
Michaela:	A hornpipe by Handel.
Atarah:	Is it an easy piece to play?
Michaela:	Well, when you start playing it, it's hard, and when you practise and practise, it gradually gets easier until you get used to it.
Atarah:	That's a good lesson for the children who are listening. How much practising do you do?
Michaela:	Every other day, I do half an hour.
Atarah:	All at one time? The trumpet's hard work, isn't it?
Michaela:	Well, it is hard work, but I take a break and come back to it.
Atarah:	You mean you go and watch the telly and then come back. At what age did you start playing the trumpet?
Michaela:	Well, actually I started playing the violin when I was $5\frac{1}{2}$. Then when I was 6, I saw a television programme of Jack Parnell and his Big Band and I just liked the sound of the trumpet ... so I decided to learn it.
Atarah:	But you were much too small at 6. I mean, your hands weren't big enough, and you hadn't got enough puff, had you?
Michaela:	Well, I had enough puff, somebody had to hold the bell up for me.
Atarah:	While you practised, somebody supported the end of the instrument?

Michaela: Yes.

Atarah: Who was that? Your Dad or your Mum?

Michaela: Well, at first, I practised with a boy at the Centre. And he had to hold it up while I was blowing in it.

Atarah: What centre was this?

Michaela: Liverpool Youth Music Centre.

Atarah: That's where you started learning the trumpet?

Michaela: Yes. When I started to practise, I started with the mouthpiece first, to get used to the feel of it.

Atarah: And don't you get dizzy from blowing?

Michaela: Well, sometimes when you play for quite a long time you get dizzy, and that's the time when you are supposed to stop and have a rest.

Atarah: How long did it take you before you could play a real tune on the trumpet?

Michaela: It took quite a few weeks. I started off with the scale of C major, the easiest scale, and it gradually builded it up . . .

Atarah: Until you could play a whole tune. I see. And then what happened? Did you start taking exams and all that sort of thing?

Michaela: Well, I played bits from the *Tune A Day* book first, for fun, not for serious things like exams. I got on to harder pieces when we started to think about exams. On trumpet, you start on Grade 3. It was quite a long time before I took Grade 3, but I took it and I passed it.

Atarah: That's fantastic, and what grade have you got now?

Michaela: Grade 5.

Atarah: Grade 5 at nine! That's exceptionally good. Because even things like the aural training are hard. You've got to learn to train your ear as well as playing the trumpet. Do you enjoy taking exams or do you get nervous?

Michaela: Well, sometimes the thought of it first makes you get nervous.

Atarah: Your stomach goes funny, doesn't it?

Michaela: Yes. You get butterflies.

Atarah: And what about playing with other children? Do you play in orchestras?

Michaela: Yes, I play in a school orchestra on violin and on trumpet. I play in the Liverpool Youth Festival Orchestra which is concert music. It's a symphony orchestra, and I play first trumpet.

Atarah:	Do you play any other sort of music?
Michaela:	Well, I play in a brass band and a jazz band.
Atarah:	Busy girl! Any other kind of music?
Michaela:	I play in a band – another band – which is a concert band.
Atarah:	You mean a kind of military band. There's no violins?
Michaela:	No violins – there's woodwind, brass and percussion – sometimes timpani.
Atarah:	For a nine-year-old, that's a lot of places to play. Doesn't it distract a bit from your school-work?
Michaela:	Well, sometimes, I should miss it out because of my homework. I do go to the Youth Music Centre for fun and so my homework should come first for school.
Atarah:	So playing really is a fun thing for you?
Michaela:	Yes, it's very nice.
Atarah:	Can you play us a piece – not like the Handel piece which is classical music – something different from your jazz or band world.
Michaela:	Yes. I'll play "Smoke Gets In Your Eyes".

(MUSIC – MICHAELA PLAYS)

Atarah:	That was great. It's a marvellous instrument the trumpet, all these different kinds of music you can play, isn't it? What's your favourite kind of music?
Michaela:	Jazz.
Atarah:	Jazz? And who do you like best? Do you have any favourites?
Michaela:	Well, Count Basie and Glen Miller. I like them, because it's good fun to play and it's nice.

EXTRACT 2: Rachel, aged 10

Learning the violin for one year.
Grade 1.

(MUSIC – RACHEL PLAYS)

Atarah:	What a beautiful sound you make, Rachel. How long have you been playing the violin?

Rachel: About a year.

Atarah: Do you enjoy it?

Rachel: Yes, very much. It makes a nice sound, nicer than any other instrument, I think.

Atarah: And how much practising do you do a day?

Rachel: About half an hour.

Atarah: Do you enjoy practising?

Rachel: No, not really.

Atarah: Oh, why not?

Rachel: Because you have to play the same things all the time.

Atarah: Well, if you didn't play the same things all the time you wouldn't get better. When you practise, do you concentrate on making a good sound all the time.

Rachel: Yes, and the bowing.

Atarah: How did you learn at the beginning?

Rachel: Holding the violin and holding the bow, getting it to go straight on the strings . . .

Atarah: How do you mean? Keeping the bow straight on the strings?

Rachel: Well, it slides up and down sometimes and goes over the bridge. So you have to stop it from moving up and down.

Atarah: Is that difficult?

Rachel: Yes.

Atarah: Doesn't the bow tend to bounce up and down on the strings when you're first learning?

Rachel: Yes, it does, but you have to learn to keep your hand which is holding the bow, at the right angle all the time.

Atarah: Did you mind learning that sort of thing?

Rachel: Not really. I wanted to get it good, so I wouldn't have to concentrate on it later.

Atarah: That's a good reason. Why did you start the violin?

Rachel: Because in school they were testing you and we had the opportunity to start – and I came out one of the top in the ear test . . . so I started.

Atarah: You started to learn at school, in a class lesson?

Rachel: Yes.

Atarah: And then what happened?

Rachel: I got on so well, I changed to a private teacher.

Atarah: And you got Grade I terribly quickly, didn't you?

Rachel: Yes, after twelve lessons.

Atarah: How many marks did you get?

Rachel: 136.

Atarah: Out of 150. That's very good after twelve lessons. What about your aural tests, did you get full marks for those?

Rachel: Well, no, not quite.

Atarah: You are quite small for ten, Rachel. Do you play a full-size violin yet?

Rachel: No, just a half-size.

Atarah: Is it your own instrument?

Rachel: No, I borrowed it from my own teacher.

Atarah: When you are bigger, you'll change to a three-quarter size. Will you buy that or will you borrow that, if possible?

Rachel: We've borrowed one from our friend – it's not actually in working order – the teacher is going to string it up and get it in tune.

Atarah: Do you play with any other people yet, or just at home on your own?

Rachel: Just at home.

Atarah: Your Mummy plays an instrument, doesn't she?

Rachel: Yes, the piano and the recorder.

Atarah: And does she accompany you?

Rachel: Yes. On the piano, while I practise.

Atarah: Is that nice?

Rachel: Yes – it seems to put the touch to it.

Atarah: (Laughs) It does help, having a Mummy who can help you practise on the violin.

Rachel: Yes.

Atarah: Did she help you from the very beginning?

Rachel: Yes.

Atarah: What did she do?

Rachel: I told her what Mr. Shaw, my teacher, told me and then she helped me.

Atarah: How good do you want to get at the violin?

Rachel: Professional.

Atarah: Why?

Rachel: It would just be nice.

Atarah: Nice to do it for a living one day?

Rachel: Yes.

Atarah: Ah, well, if you go on making such a beautiful sound, perhaps one day you will be a professional violinist.

EXTRACT 3: Susannah, aged 10

Learning the piano for two years.
Grade 1.

(MUSIC – SUSANNAH PLAYS)

Atarah: Thank you, Susie. That was one of the pieces for Grade 1. When are you taking Grade 2?

Susannah: This term.

Atarah: Have you taken any exams yet?

Susannah: I've taken four exams so far. Step 1, Step 2, Step 3, and Grade 1. They are very easy exams, but I think they're quite important, because it proves you've got somewhere. It makes all the work seem worth while.

Atarah: How much practising do you do?

Susannah: Half-hour at least.

Atarah: What age were you when you started playing the piano?

Susannah: Properly?

Atarah: Yes.

Susannah: About eight.

Atarah: And why did you start?

Susannah: Because I used to go to my Gran's, and every time I went there, she had this piano, and I used to play on it ... it was just really nice to play on it.

Atarah: And what age were you when you first tried the piano at Gran's?

Susannah: About three.

Atarah: It took five years to get a piano of your own! Why did it take so long?

Susannah: Well, 'cos my Mum and Dad didn't think I'd practise on it, you know, and I'd just neglect it and not play it.

Atarah: So they waited till you were older?

Susannah: Yes.

Atarah: Do you have any problems reading music at the piano?

Susannah: No, it's quite easy really.

Atarah: Are you good at Maths, because that helps a bit.

Susannah: Yes.

Atarah: What sort of things do you find hard, though, on the piano?

Susannah:	Well, sometimes concentrating on both hands, 'cos you can get your right hand nearly perfect and your left hand is all over the place. When it comes to the place where you can't get your right hand perfectly you have to concentrate on both of them very hard.
Atarah:	Now tell me, what about this other instrument you've brought for me to hear today: a piano accordion. Isn't it very heavy?
Susannah:	Well, some of them are and some of them aren't.
Atarah:	Which are you going to play for us, the heavy one or the light one?
Susannah:	The light one.
Atarah:	How long have you had a piano accordion?
Susannah:	Not very long. I don't know really, but not very long.
Atarah:	But how did you get hold of one – it's a strange instrument for a child to play.
Susannah:	Well, it was second-hand. My Dad got it from a second-hand shop.
Atarah:	What do the left and right hands do? Which one has the tune?
Susannah:	The right hand has the tune and the left hand just plays chords.
Atarah:	You mean these funny buttons. And how many buttons have you got on the small piano-accordion?
Susannah:	Twelve.
Atarah:	And how many on a big one?
Susannah:	One hundred and twenty.
Atarah:	Well, let's hear a little tune. Play us "Jingle Bells" on your small piano accordion.

(MUSIC – SUSANNAH PLAYS)

Atarah:	Thank you, Susie, that's very nice. The left hand is not only using the buttons, it seems to be pushing things in and out like a bellows. Isn't it hard work?
Susannah:	Well, it's very hard work at first, but you get used to it and so it just comes automatically after a while.
Atarah:	Do you have lessons?
Susannah:	No. I teach myself. It's quite hard.
Atarah:	What about the piano? Regular lessons?
Susannah:	Yes.

Atarah:	Are they the high spots of the week, your piano lessons?
Susannah:	Yes, they are, really. You know they're just very nice – Mr. Partington, the man who teaches me, is very nice.
Atarah:	Is it important, that each week you've got somebody to play to, to see if you are improving or not?
Susannah:	Yes, and he tells you all your mistakes.
Atarah:	Now what's the importance of your playing the piano accordion? What do you want to do with it one day, when you get proficient at it?
Susannah:	Well, one day I hope to be in a pop group.
Atarah:	On the piano accordion?
Susannah:	Yeah!

EXTRACT 4: Jane, aged 11

Learned clarinet in class situation for six months.
No grade.

(MUSIC – JANE PLAYS)

Atarah:	Tell me, Jane, you're eleven and you've only been playing six months properly now. Do you enjoy it?
Jane:	Yes. When I was just playing it by myself and I didn't have lessons at school, I got very lonely, you know, and I thought "Oh, this is a bit boring." But when I got to school and started playing with other people, I found it was a very good instrument. Unlike the piano because you can play with lots of other people, and the clarinet's a very popular instrument now.
Atarah:	Yes, it is. How many clarinets have you got in this local band you play in?
Jane:	There's about twenty clarinets and it's run by the teacher who comes to school to give us clarinet lessons.
Atarah:	So you enjoy your orchestra?
Jane:	Yes. I like being together with my new friends.
Atarah:	And is the music easy?

Jane:	No. That's the problem. If I know the tune, it's all right. But if we're playing a tune I don't know . . . like, if I'm a second clarinet . . . I get lost.
Atarah:	How do you mean: get lost?
Jane:	Well . . . I can't read the music.
Atarah:	You mean, you can't read the notes?
Jane:	Of course, I can read notes, that's easy. But I never understand how the others know when to play.
Atarah:	Then you don't really understand rhythm. How do you manage during the lessons at school?
Jane:	That's easy. My friend's very good so I just follow her.
Atarah:	But it's really hard when you can't follow someone, isn't it? Can your Mum or Dad help you?
Jane:	They don't know anything about music. But my brother plays in this rock-and-roll group. It's great.

(Note: Gave up playing after a further six months, unable to cope with rhythm. Fell in love with ponies, instead!)

EXTRACT 5: Dave, aged 13

Learning the cornet for eighteen months.
Grade 3.

(MUSIC – DAVE PLAYS)

Atarah:	Well, that was Dave Roberts playing "Rock Around The Clock" with one of his mates on guitar. Is it good fun playing with other people, Dave?
Dave:	Yes, it's great.
Atarah:	Why?
Dave:	Well, you've got to have co-ordination, and do all your notes right.
Atarah:	You mean, the fun of playing with somebody else is that you can test yourself?

Dave:	That's right – yes. Playing with other people is great. You try to outdo everybody else.
Atarah:	Competitive fellow! How many cornets have you got in your school band?
Dave:	There's two firsts – me and this other lad.
Atarah:	Is he as good as you?
Dave:	He's better than me.
Atarah:	So you've got to outdo him, haven't you?
Dave:	Yeah – well he's leaving next year, so I'm all right. And there's three seconds.
Atarah:	What are they like?
Dave:	Rubbish.
Atarah:	Why did you start the cornet?
Dave:	Well, the school music teacher asked, you know, if I wanted to start an instrument and I said yes. Well, he said, "What do you want to play?". And I said: "Something like a cornet or something like that."
Atarah:	Why did you choose that?
Dave:	I don't know. I just like the cornet sound.
Atarah:	Do you mean, when you hear it on the radio, say in brass bands?
Dave:	Yeah – and in jazz.
Atarah:	But they don't use the cornet in jazz.
Dave:	No, they use the trumpet.
Atarah:	So you mean, you like the sound of a brass instrument, and a cornet was available?
Dave:	No. A trumpet was available, but the mouthpiece had got stuck in the end, and when we took it to the metalwork teacher to get it out, it split, see. So, it had to go away to be repaired, and I had to use the cornet.
Atarah:	I see. So you started the cornet about a year ago. What sort of things did you do in your first lessons?
Dave:	Just getting your notes right.
Atarah:	Could you read music before you started?
Dave:	No, I never read music before I started my cornet.
Atarah:	Was it difficult or not?
Dave:	Well, some lessons, you can do about seven tunes, and the other times you can only do about one or two.
Atarah:	And then what happened after that on the cornet?
Dave:	Oh, well then, I got into the band.
Atarah:	At school?

Dave: Yeah – school band. And oh, then I went from second to first, and played along with the first, and then I went to this other band.

Atarah: What's that like?

Dave: Oh, it's great, you know. It has all saxophones and clarinets and flutes and things like that, and oboes, and you know, they are really good players.

Atarah: So you've improved a lot, have you, since you've done that?

Dave: Oh yeah.

Atarah: And what's going to happen now then?

Dave: Well, I think I'm going to change to the trumpet, and then I'm just going to see what goes on from there.

Atarah: How much practising do you do?

Dave: About 15 minutes a night. And then at school every dinner time, and band practices.

Atarah: How often do you have band practices?

Dave: Twice a week.

Atarah: What else do you do at dinner-time?

Dave: Oh, just go in and play my cornet.

Atarah: In a practice room?

Dave: A music room.

Atarah: Well, you go to a marvellous new comprehensive school. I'm told that at lunch-time, if you walk down the street, you can hear electric guitars, bass guitars, trumpets, cornets, belting out. But, the disadvantage of being in a new school is that there are not many senior boys playing musical instruments, are there?

Dave: Not many, no.

Atarah: So we need youngsters like you in a new school to build up the pattern of music. What do you want to do when you leave school?

Dave: Well, I want to join the Navy. My friend's in the Navy and it sounds fantastic, you know, the life and everything. And I can play music for a hobby.

EXTRACT 6: Helen, aged 12

Learning saxophone for 2 years.
Grade: No exams for this instrument.
Notional Grade 5

(MUSIC – HELEN PLAYS "GIRL FROM IPONEMA")

Atarah: Where do you play that kind of music?

Helen: In the Liverpool Jazz Workshop. It's a jazz band. We play Glen Miller stuff and Count Basie.

Atarah: What combination of instruments are in the band?

Helen: Trumpet, saxes, drums, guitar, got a bass guitar, piano.

Atarah: Is it physically difficult to play the tenor sax? It's a very large instrument really.

Helen: You just have to practise. Just have to practise and practise.

Atarah: How much practising do you do?

Helen: About two hours a day.

Atarah: About two hours a day! What do you do? Scales and fast passages?

Helen: Not all the time ... about half an hour of scales and things.

Atarah: Well, let's hear how fast you play after two hours a day of practice.

(MUSIC – HELEN PLAYS FAST SCALES)

Atarah: Gosh, that's great. What else do you practise?

Helen: Just tunes, from the jazz workshop you know. I bring the pad home and practise over the tunes that we are going to play.

Atarah: What about improvising? Do you improvise, yet? By that I mean not playing exactly what's written but making it up as you go along.

Helen: A bit. I do a bit of twelve-bar blues.

Atarah: Is that difficult?

Helen: Yes ... You have to think about all the chords and what notes are in the chords.

Atarah: You mean if you are playing in the chord of C you've got to work out that you can improvise on C, E and G.

Helen: Yes. But when you've practised it and you are really good, you don't have to think about it; you just hear the chord and you automatically play the notes.

Atarah: You haven't got to that level yet?

Helen: No, not yet.

Atarah: You will do. Do you feel you've a flair for improvising?

Helen: Yes, I will do eventually.

Atarah: But there's no short cuts. It isn't, like some people think, an easy thing to do, to play jazz. You've got to learn and work at it.

Helen: Yes, you've got to work very hard.

Atarah: Why did you start playing the sax?

Helen: Well, I've played the piano since I was five and Dad's always been a great fan of Charlie Parker (and sort of I'd grown up to like his playing) and I just went up to him one day and said: "I want to play the sax." And he brought me a very old alto sax.

Atarah: Most children start on the alto sax which is smaller, but why have you taken up the tenor sax?

Helen: Well, I did start on the alto, but it was only for a couple of months.

Atarah: You didn't like it?

Helen: No, it was very old, the one that Dad bought me and very hard to blow.

Atarah: Why didn't you buy a new, easy alto sax?

Helen: I don't know. Dad just bought it. I didn't know he was going to get it.

Atarah: Thank you. Time for a record, now. What would you like us to play?

Helen: Stan Getz – playing "Desafinado".

EXTRACT 7: Sarah, aged 9

Playing recorder for three years.
No grade.

Atarah: Why did you start playing the recorder?

Sarah: Because I liked the other people playing it, at school.

Atarah: And did your Mummy buy you the first recorder?

Sarah:	No. My Grandma did.
Atarah:	How did you start playing? Did you learn at home, or did you learn at school?
Sarah:	I learnt at school with a class teacher.
Atarah:	How many children all together?
Sarah:	About twelve.
Atarah:	Did you start off by learning to read music?
Sarah:	No. We had the notes all at the beginning.
Atarah:	How do you mean? Instead of writing B in musical notation, you actually had a letter B written down?
Sarah:	Yes.
Atarah:	But you don't read that way now.
Sarah:	No.
Atarah:	You read music very easily.
Sarah:	Yes.
Atarah:	How much practising do you do on the recorder?
Sarah:	About quarter-of-an-hour, because I have to practise my piano as well.
Atarah:	And when do you practise, in the morning before you go to school?
Sarah:	Yes, I practise it in bed.
Atarah:	In bed. That's a very good advantage of learning the recorder: you can play it in bed because it doesn't disturb anybody.
Sarah:	It disturbs Craig.
Atarah:	Who's Craig?
Sarah:	My brother.
Atarah:	Poor old Craig. Does he disturb you?
Sarah:	He makes silly noises in the morning.
Atarah:	That's typical of brothers, isn't it? Now, you have another recorder. What's this one called?
Sarah:	Treble.
Atarah:	A treble. Is it more difficult to play than a descant?
Sarah:	Yes. Because it's got different fingering and you have to blow harder.
Atarah:	Well, let's hear you play on your treble recorder now, please.

(MUSIC – SARAH PLAYS "GREENSLEEVES")

Atarah:	I like the sound of a treble recorder – I think it is lovely. Do

	you play with other children at school?
Sarah:	Yes.
Atarah:	Which recorder do you play with other children?
Sarah:	Well, we play the descant recorder.
Atarah:	All together in one group?
Sarah:	Yes.
Atarah:	And do you play in the school orchestra as well?
Sarah:	Yes.
Atarah:	On what instrument?
Sarah:	The glockenspiel.
Atarah:	You play a lot of instruments, don't you? Now you've told me that there's another instrument that you really want to play. What's that?
Sarah:	A flute.
Atarah:	Why do you want to play the flute?
Sarah:	'Cos I've heard you playing it in the Band. It's got a nice sound, it's got different fingering. It's a change from the descant recorder.
Atarah:	Yes. You mean it would be interesting to learn something else. Well, let's see how you do for the very first time on the flute. I'll give you my head joint, and let's see if you can make a sound, because if you are going to take up the flute, first of all we've got to check that you have the right-shaped mouth.

(Note: Sarah transferred to the flute (a little young), is having regular lessons and making good progress.)

EXTRACT 8: Rick, aged 13
Learning classical guitar for fifteen months.
Grade 3.

Atarah:	This week's young guitarist is unusual in that he plays both the classical and the electric guitar. First of all, let's hear him play his classical guitar.

(MUSIC – RICK PLAYS CARCASSI MINUET)

Atarah: Thank you, Rick. Do you enjoy playing the guitar?

Rick: Yes, I do. I find it very satisfying.

Atarah: Is it a difficult instrument to play?

Rick: Very, yes.

Atarah: Why very?

Rick: Because you have to get both hands co-ordinating in different ways.

Atarah: Ah, you mean the left hand and right hand have got different things to do. What about your fingers? Now, I've often known professional guitarists who have terrible problems when they break a nail or when they hurt one of their fingers. Have you found that already?

Rick: Yes, yes.

Atarah: Does it affect your sports or your cycling or any of your hobbies?

Rick: Yes, you have to be very careful when you do. I've stopped skateboarding, you know, till I've taken the exam.

Atarah: Which grade?

Rick: Grade 3.

Atarah: Did you pass Grade 1 and Grade 2?

Rick: Well, I passed Grade 1, but I missed Grade 2 out.

Atarah: Why?

Rick: Because I was too good.

Atarah: Oh, I see. Well, if you are working for an exam, do you work every day doing the same sort of thing?

Rick: Yes, you do scales, arpeggios to get your hands warmed up and supple, and then you start doing the pieces.

Atarah: How long do you practise your scales for each day?

Rick: About fifteen minutes.

Atarah: Fifteen minutes. And how long do you practise all together?

Rick: About forty minutes.

Atarah: When you first started the guitar, did you practise for that long?

Rick: Oh no, nothing like that. Sometimes it was only about fifteen minutes.

Atarah: Only! I think that if every child practised every day for fifteen minutes, they'd all improve, would you say that?

Rick:	Yes. Until you got to a certain standard. Then you find it very hard.
Atarah:	Do you think forty minutes is going to be enough for you, now?
Rick:	Yes. Until I pass Grade 3 and get on to a different grade. Then it will take an hour a day for Grade 5.
Atarah:	Is all the hard work worth while?
Rick:	Yes, because you can hear yourself improving all the time. And, anyway, it's given me something to do with my spare time.
Atarah:	I think that's a very important reason for playing a musical instrument. Now, you also play another instrument. It's the electric guitar. People think the electric guitar is very similar to the classical guitar, but it has a very different technique, hasn't it?
Rick:	The technique on the left hand's not different, no. But the right hand, you have to use a plectrum.
Atarah:	Ah, a plectrum, instead of your nails. Well, can we hear you play your electric guitar now? Will you improvise something . . . play something that comes from your head?

(MUSIC – RICK IMPROVISES)

Atarah:	That's very, very different from the sound and the approach of the classical guitar. What's the basic difference?
Rick:	You're much freer to express yourself because you are not playing somebody else's music, you are playing your own music. No fixed pattern to it.
Atarah:	How much do you play on the electric guitar every day?
Rick:	About the same as the classical, now. I used to play it a lot more.
Atarah:	What do you want to be?
Rick:	A musician, I think.
Atarah:	A musician. How do you mean, a musician? Do you want to play like I did in a symphony orchestra? No, you can't, because there's no guitars in symphony orchestras.
Rick:	Well, I think I want to play solo, lead soloist really. I'd like to have a group of my own and play lead guitar.

EXTRACT 9: Heather, aged 15

Playing mandolin for four years.

Grade: No exams for this instrument.

Notional Grade 8

Atarah: We're recording this interview at the Fretted Instruments Festival where Heather has been winning all the solo and group classes. Are competitions exciting?

Heather: Very. They are the only chance a mandolinist has to ... well, perform in front of a critical audience, because there are no examinations for mandolinists, yet.

Atarah: So this is your one chance to assess yourself. Are you nervous?

Heather: I'm very nervous, yes.

Atarah: What does it feel like being nervous? Describe it.

Heather: Well, you feel as though both hands are shaking but not in time with the music.

Atarah: I know the feeling. Why did you start the mandolin?

Heather: I once heard a recording of Troise and his Mandoliers. They were a famous mandolin orchestra quite a few years ago now, and they finished. I liked the sound of the instrument and decided from then that that's what I'd like to play.

Atarah: Did you play anything else before?

Heather: No, I didn't play any instruments before the mandolin. I couldn't read music at all and we didn't do music at primary school.

Atarah: So you have to read music to play the mandolin ...

Heather: Not in the initial stages but certainly if you're going to do it seriously, you do have to.

Atarah: What sort of pieces are you playing?

Heather: Most of the time, we play specially arranged pieces of classical music. But the mandolin is adaptable to any music.

Atarah: And the main thing is to learn to use your right hand, with the plectrum on the strings. Isn't that the hardest thing?

Heather: Yes, that's really the most difficult technique. It's referred to as the tremolo and it has to be smooth and sustained.

Atarah: How much practising do you do?

Heather: Well, I do about four hours every night.
Atarah: Oh, that explains it. I thought you were fantastic when I heard you play. Are you very serious about it?
Heather: Oh yes, if there's anything I could do to further people's interest in the mandolin, I'd do it.
Atarah: I think that's most unusual. Are there many players of your age on the mandolin?
Heather: Well, there are some, but there's more elderly people play it.
Atarah: You're getting quite fanatical about it?
Heather: Oh yes, I am.
Atarah: How much did your instrument cost?
Heather: This instrument is a Domalia mandolin, it's a very old mandolin, it's dated inside, 1900, and it cost £150. It was a collector's piece when we bought it and it belonged to a collection by Philip J. Bone who did write a history about the instrument but, when he died, his daughter sold off the collection and this is one of the instruments.
Atarah: You only play the mandolin. You're not bothering with any other musical instrument?
Heather: Oh, the mandolin is my thing for life but I do occasionally play the oboe.
Atarah: What are you going to do when you leave school?
Heather: Well, I haven't decided yet but I'm trying to do something with the mandolin. I'd love to do that.
Atarah: So if you can discover a lot about the history you can do one-man-mandolin-girl shows or . . . if you see what I mean.
Heather: I hope so . . .
Atarah: Do you play in any bands at the moment?
Heather: Yes, I play for the Granada Mandoliers, we practise in Wallasey. It's a group of fourteen people, we have six mandolinists, three guitars and a piano accordion, a bass guitar and a glockenspiel.
Atarah: Is it fun?
Heather: Oh, it's great fun.
Atarah: Would you recommend other children to learn the mandolin, or is it something you come across and it just suits you?
Heather: Well, it suits me personally but then I tend to be a perfectionist. Still, I would advise people to try it.

Atarah: How are you a perfectionist?

Heather: Well, the mandolin has to be really played. You know, you really have to put your heart and soul into it to produce the tone because most people just sort of sit and play it and think they're making the sound and yet ... it just sort of brings a superficial sound out of it.

Atarah: That's interesting, because I've been sitting here listening to ... well, hundreds of mandolinists ... and you were the one person who struck me as having outstanding life and energy in your playing. You mean, in order to make the kind of quality that you make you've had to really work hard at it?

Heather: Oh yes, you really have to work and you find at the end of a long practice session that you are physically exhausted, quite honestly.

EXTRACT 10: Philip, aged 15

Learning bass guitar for eighteen months.
Grade: No exams for this instrument.

Philip: The first instrument I learned was acoustic guitar. I started on that about six years ago.

Atarah: And what did you play on the acoustic guitar?

Philip: Mainly chords and folk songs.

Atarah: So you never actually learnt to read music?

Philip: No, I didn't.

Atarah: And why did you change on to the bass guitar?

Philip: Someone asked if we'd start off a group for the school and we wanted a rhythm section. We tried it with drums, but it didn't seem to fit in, like, so we decided to try with a bass, and I took up the bass guitar.

Atarah: And are you pleased you took up the bass guitar?

Philip: Yes, I am.

Atarah: Does it suit you really?

Philip: In a way, yes. 'Cos I always like keeping the rhythm and the beat in the band.

Atarah:	You're not frustrated about never playing the tune?
Philip:	Not really, no.
Atarah:	What sort of things do you practise on the bass guitar?
Philip:	Mainly rhythms, chord-notes and tunes, and scales – roots and fifths and octaves, you know.
Atarah:	So you do basic technical practice all the time. How much do you do a day?
Philip:	Up to four hours a day.
Atarah:	That's a tremendous amount. Do you listen to yourself very critically as you practise?
Philip:	How do you mean?
Atarah:	Well, if you play a piano or, say, a classical guitar, you can see yourself improving each week, because each week there's a more difficult piece to learn. But this isn't the case on the bass guitar, is it? There's no repertoire.
Philip:	No, as you say, it would be on a normal guitar, like when you are playing classical because it will build up to harder things. On a bass, you more or less just play one thing after another, keeping the normal beat.
Atarah:	You don't get bored?
Philip:	Not really, no.
Atarah:	Well, let's hear you playing one of your own sort of typical bass parts that you play with your jazz groups. Let's hear it first of all on the bass guitar with the amplifier.

(MUSIC – PHILIP PLAYS)

Atarah:	Thank you. Where did you get the amplifier?
Philip:	I made it myself. It's a small practice amplifier.
Atarah:	Does it make a lot of noise?
Philip:	It's 25 watts.
Atarah:	So that doesn't drive the family crazy?
Philip:	No.
Atarah:	Have you ever played the classical bass instrument – the double-bass?
Philip:	Actually I did start off with a double-bass, but I didn't really like it because it was a big thing to carry around, and obviously I would have to learn to read bass clef in order to play it.
Atarah:	What about now, are you going to try and learn the bass clef?

Philip: I have actually started to read bass clef . . .

Atarah: Why do you consider it necessary to learn to read music?

Philip: Well, I'm hoping to go into music professionally, when I leave school – teaching bass guitar and acoustic guitar.

Atarah: It would be marvellous if you teach the bass guitar because there are surprisingly few teachers of bass guitar who can actually read music, aren't there? How will you go about becoming a bass guitar teacher?

Philip: Well, hopefully with a lot of help from people around here.

Atarah: Have you got a good set-up at school?

Philip: We have peripatetic teachers coming into school. We don't actually have a bass guitar teacher, but we have an electric guitar teacher who did play the bass.

Atarah: So, in other words, you get a good musical background from school. What about 'O' levels and that sort of thing?

Philip: Well, next year I shall be taking CSE and then 'O' levels and then 'A' levels.

Atarah: And you want to do music?

Philip: I do, yes.

Atarah: And then after that?

Philip: There could be a place for me in a centre – a music centre. I want to be a peripatetic teacher.

Atarah: Would you have to go to music college ... or not necessarily?

Philip: I'll have to do two years at a high school to get 'A' levels and I might go to the Music College to take my teaching certificate.

Atarah: So you've got it all pretty clearly marked out – what you want to do?

Philip: Hopefully.

Atarah: Don't you want to play in a group?

Philip: I do, yes. I want to get experience of dance bands, jazz groups, classical guitar.

Atarah: What about the pop world?

Philip: I'm not really that way inclined to pop music.

Atarah: What way are you inclined?

Philip: Jazz and the contemporary music.

(Note: For this fifteen-year-old, four hours practising a day can only be for personal therapy.)

EXTRACT 11: Vera, aged 19

Learning double-bass for four years.
Grade VIII+

(MUSIC – VERA PLAYS "THE ELEPHANT" BY
SAINT SAENS)

Atarah: What a beautiful sound, Vera. You don't often expect to hear the bass sounding as nice as that. It's very unusual to see a woman playing the bass. Why did you start playing?

Vera: Well, I played the clarinet to begin with and I wanted a second instrument. I couldn't play the flute so I took the double-bass.

Atarah: How do you mean you couldn't play the flute?

Vera: Well, at school we didn't have enough instruments to go round and as I already had one school instrument, I had to give way and take up the bass instead.

Atarah: You mean that, as happens so often, they said: "We need a double-bass player for the orchestra. It's you!"

Vera: Yes ... I was a big girl and that was it.

Atarah: Do you regret playing the bass at all?

Vera: Not at all. It's been a real experience, playing the bass. I've met a lot of nice people. It's good fun.

Atarah: I've never thought the bass was fun. Imagine lugging it around. Isn't it heavy?

Vera: Yes, but you don't see owt more stupid than somebody lugging a bass about, do you? ...

Atarah: Say that again?

Vera: You don't see anyone ... anything any funnier than someone carrying a bass around.

Atarah: (*Laughs*) You can tell this lass comes from the North. But, seriously, how *do* you cope with carrying a bass around?

Vera: Well, before I could drive, I had to get me Dad to take me about in the car, but now I just borrow the car from Dad.

Atarah: And if you can't, how do you manage on the buses?

Vera: I take it on the train but never on the buses.

Atarah: I see. And do you want to take it up professionally?

Vera: Yes.

Atarah: What's it going to be like as a profession?

Vera: Very difficult, I would think.

Atarah:	Why?
Vera:	Well, there aren't many women in for a start. There's a lot of resistance to women bass-players. Partly because physically it's challenging, mentally it's challenging, everything is challenging about it ... And the men in orchestra bass sections don't want women to get in.
Atarah:	I know what you mean. I was one of the first women Principals and that took a lot of doing, believe me. How old do you think is the best age to start playing the bass?
Vera:	About 13 or 14. If you've got large enough hands and you are tall enough ... and you've got to be strong.
Atarah:	Well, would you say honestly that you have no doubts about playing what most people would think of as the least important instrument in the string section?
Vera:	No, not at all.
Atarah:	Recommend it for others?
Vera:	Yes, yes, anyone with a good sense of humour.

EXTRACT 12: John, aged 17

Playing bagpipes for five years.
Grade: No exams for this instrument.
Notional Grade VI +

Atarah:	The sound of the bagpipes is rather a specialist taste. A lot of people don't like the noise. They think it sounds a bit like a gone-off oboe. But I find the more you listen to the bagpipes, the more interesting they become. Now, let's listen to today's young player who comes from near Edinburgh. First of all he's going to play for us a sort of medley. It's a hornpipe and a strathspey (which is a Highland dance) and a reel – all mixed into one. Och aye!

(MUSIC – JOHN PLAYS)

Atarah:	That was great. Was it tiring?
John:	It was a little, yes.

Atarah: How do you mean, a little? You look completely exhausted.

John: Well, it varies from . . . with the piper and his pipes. If the pipes are going well, it's easy, but if the bag's leaking air, then it's very hard work.

Atarah: Why did you start playing the bagpipes?

John: Well, it's been running in the family for quite a few generations. My grandfather was a piper. My father's a pipe major in the army. He's at present instructing at the Army School of piping at Edinburgh Castle.

Atarah: Did he teach you?

John: No, he didn't actually. No, I . . . it's . . . I don't know how other people feel about it, but I think it's quite difficult for a father to teach his son, and do it properly.

Atarah: Yes.

John: Or rather, it's more difficult for the son to accept being taught by his father.

Atarah: I don't know how many children listening have had this same experience. So you didn't want to learn from your father. How did you start?

John: I didn't really have much choice. He thought it best. He put me on to one of his friends, a piper that was in the band that he was in charge of at that time.

Atarah: And how old were you then?

John: I was eight years old at the time.

Atarah: Did you start on the full set of bagpipes, or what?

John: We started on the practice chanter. It requires a lot of practice to become proficient at the chanter.

Atarah: And do you read music or do you play from ear?

John: Read music.

Atarah: Straight music, like I read on the flute?

John: Yeah.

Atarah: Just the same?

John: Oh, it doesn't vary in keys. There are no sharps and flats on the pipes.

Atarah: So you started practising on the chanter at eight. When did you transfer to the full bagpipes?

John: I never touched the bagpipes till I was ten.

Atarah: And do you play on your own when you're a child, or do you start playing with other people straight away?

John: Well, I went to boarding-school when I was nine, and for the first two years, there was a choice of doing piping, drumming or Highland dancing. The boarding-school was in Scotland.

Atarah: We gathered that much!

John: I think there was about thirty or forty young lads joined all at the same time. And they split up into whatever they decided to do, apart from their normal schooling, of course. There was a band there, and there was a continuous supply of young pipers coming up all the time.

Atarah: So you played at home, on your own at school, you practised, and you played in the band. Would you recommend a kid to take up the bagpipes?

John: If he's keen, yes.

Atarah: And what would you say was the worst or most difficult thing about it?

John: The impression that's given about the bagpipes, things that a person might hear before they attempt to learn them, such as taking a lot of wind and making an awful noise and what not. It can be very off-putting.

Atarah: And have you finished learning yet?

John: Oh no. A lot to go yet. It's an unusual instrument in that the player has to have an excellent knowledge of how the actual instrument works, and how to service it. Maintain it and what not, even construct it really. It's a lifetime's work if you want to be really good.

Playing with others: flutes (above), baritone horns (below)

Index